STORIES I TELL MY PATIENTS

101 Myths, Metaphors, Fables & Tall Tales for Eating Disorders Recovery

ARNOLD ANDERSEN, MD
WITH LEIGH COHN, MAT, CEDS

D1468973

gürze books

Stories I Tell My Patients
101 Myths, Metaphors, Fables & Tall Tales for Eating Disorders Recovery

©2016 Arnold Andersen and Leigh Cohn

All rights reserved. Portions of this book were previously published in *Eating Disorders: The Journal of Treatment and Prevention*.

Printed in the United States of America.

No part of this book may be used or reproduced in any manner whatsoever without written permission.

Gürze Books
P.O. Box 2238
Carlsbad, CA 92018
760-434-7533
gurzebooks.com

Cover and interior design by Rob Johnson, toprotype.com

Library of Congress Cataloging-in-Publication Data

Names: Andersen, Arnold E., author. | Cohn, Leigh, author.
Title: Stories I tell my patients : 101 myths, metaphors, fables & tall tales for eating disorders recovery / Arnold Andersen, MD with Leigh Cohn, MAT, CEDS.
Description: Carlsbad, CA : Gurze Books, [2016] | Description based on print version record and CIP data provided by publisher; resource not viewed.
Identifiers: LCCN 2015045786 (print) | LCCN 2015044109 (ebook) | ISBN 9780936077833 (e-book) | ISBN 9780936077826 (paperback)
Subjects: LCSH: Eating disorders--Treatment. | BISAC: PSYCHOLOGY / Psychopathology / Eating Disorders.
Classification: LCC RC552.E18 (print) | LCC RC552.E18 A533 2016 (ebook) | DDC 616.85/2606--dc23
LC record available at http://lccn.loc.gov/2015045786

Contents

CONTENTS

Foreword

Leigh Cohn, MAT, CEDS
Editor-in-Chief
Eating Disorders: The Journal of Treatment and Prevention

"Stories I Tell My Patients" by Arnold Andersen, MD has been an intermittent feature in *Eating Disorders: The Journal of Treatment and Prevention* since our first issue in 1993. The complete set of 101 stories is collected here in one volume for the first time. Combining myth, metaphor, fable, tall tale, and inventive fantasy, they were originally intended for professionals treating eating disorders to read and share with their clients, though they can also be read and appreciated by individuals in recovery and their loved ones.

An eclectic mix, Arnold's stories are both entertaining and insightful. Some are vaguely familiar—with his own offbeat interpretations—such as the retelling of "The Emperor Has No Clothes" or Faustian deals with the devil; and, Jack and Jill appear, but instead of rolling down a hill, they are canoeing down a rapid river. There are knights in shining armor, time machines, intergalactic travelers, stories derived from Greek mythology, anorexic saints of the 16th century, and current events (a few of which may seem dated, like Hurricane Floyd or top baseball salaries of five million dollars). Most of the stories sprang from Arnold's imagination, and many were inspired by his direct interactions with patients. He introduces such characters as Tom, Dick, and Harry going camping, Muffy and Buffy sitting in judgment, and Clip and Clop plowing a field.

Inanimate objects such as buoys and thermometers carry on conversations, and descriptions of Paris reflect the author's love of that beautiful city.

In 1992, I knew Dr. Andersen's reputation as a leading eating disorders researcher and author of the book *Males and Eating Disorders,* but we'd never met. I was in the process of founding the journal and had gotten some commitments for editorial board members, as well as lining up two senior editors, Margo Maine and John Foreyt, but I needed one more. Craig Johnson gave me Dr. Andersen's number and I called him—perhaps a quaint notion in this day and age. I introduced myself and told him about this new kind of peer review journal in eating disorders that would be more clinically oriented. It would also include rotating features such as book reviews, editorials, and "How I Practice" articles. I explained that I needed a senior editor with a strong academic background, who could help me with decisions about complex research.

He immediately accepted my invitation, and then he said he had some suggestions and ideas. He created the template for our evaluation form, recruited other esteemed reviewers, and asked me if I'd be interested in printing stories therapists could tell their patients. We brainstormed the nuts and bolts: the articles would be clever and short, and each one would be followed with a "Comment" reminiscent of some Zen stories I was reading at the time. The journal's readers—primarily therapists—could use the stories in their everyday practices. I loved the concept and that it was so non-traditional for an academic journal, and thus began our collaboration.

Through the years, Arnold and I have developed a productive and enduring friendship. In addition to these stories and our journal work together, we coauthored, along with Tom Holbrook, the book *Making Weight,* have given memorable workshops together at professional conferences, and have enjoyed fascinating discussions about a wide range of subjects, from testosterone supplementation with male anorexic patients to Impressionist painting. I have tremendous respect for his intellect, creativity, and compassion, and, like each of his stories, he is absolutely one of a kind.

Typically, Arnold sends me a first draft, which needs editing. The plot is usually strong, the message solid, and the writing a bit stream of consciousness and free form. I am like the varnisher of a master's oil painting. My job is to make it shine. A few of the stories are, indeed, masterpieces, and others may leave you scratching your head. However, oftentimes the "ah-ha moment" may hit you a little later, upon further consideration. For this book, we have done some slight tweaking of the language for the sake of continuity. We've also edited potentially disturbing content that was originally written for therapists to read but now is intended for a mixed audience of professionals, families, and individuals in recovery.

Not every story is for every reader. Therefore, for this book, we've added keywords with each piece. We've also included an index of these topics with the corresponding stories. They are arranged chronologically in order of publication, because, there was no other logical structure. Readers can read through the book from beginning to end, choose stories at random, or select specific ones with keywords of interest. For example, for individuals in recovery from anorexia nervosa, that term is in the index, as well as related topics like thinness, perfectionism, family dynamics, and anxiety. Nonetheless, even if a story is unrelated to the issue at hand, it may still be entertaining and enlightening. One of my favorites is the final entry, a 2015 release titled, "Jeanette's Feast" (#101), which is a wonderful tale about full recovery and family gratitude.

Whether the person in recovery reading these stories is a Toggler or a Dimmer (#100), there are nuggets of gold here to aid them in their journey. Pick the weeds and grow flowers.

Introduction

Storytelling is an old and honored art. Great literature conveys its message to us in stories. In a way, the stories remain the same—they tell of life, love, death, birth, hope, loss, discovery, fear, quest, beauty, humor, truth, falsehood, despair, chicanery, faith, and all the other great issues of life. They can be imaginary or about real people, happenings, objects, and experiences. The bureaucratic, polysyllabic, intellectualized approach to life has always gone over peoples' heads and into the trash basket, where it belongs. And I have contributed my share to that trash basket.

Patients with eating disorders often have superficial insight they clothe in long words that do not ring true. This is especially so of young, anorexic girls who are intellectually precocious but emotionally immature. It also applies to the person with bulimic symptoms who searches for words to deal with fundamental emotions, but, never finding them, offers up instead jargon.

Some time ago, when I felt stuck with patients in psychotherapy or on rounds and found we were trading words rather than making real progress, I began to tell short stories in order to find a way around the intellectualized defenses and to get to the issues. Rational and intellectual understanding are only valuable when they ring true, and when they are joined with the emotions that go along with the ideas. All forms of communication have strengths and weaknesses. Storytelling is not meant ultimately to deal with eating disorder problems, but rather to get attention, to convey an idea, to instill a seed, to shake a complacency. No matter how old we get, we can relate to roses and bike trips, shadows, and catsup.

I hope these stories convey helpful information, and encourage others to use storytelling in their work. Maybe if we raised children with more stories of quests, heroines, noble deeds, and skinned knees, we would have fewer eating disorders. Maybe not. In the meantime, each clinical case of an eating disorder presents a challenge, and sometimes the challenge of treatment may be helped by stories.

Originally published in 1993.

1

Watering the Roses when the House is on Fire

anorexia nervosa, perfectionism, anxiety

What would you say if I told you the story of a young girl who was very good at watering the roses? One day, the house caught on fire and she was very afraid, not knowing how to put it out. She had been taught in school to leave the house promptly and call the fire department. She was told that sometimes, if the fire was very small, she could put it out safely by covering it with a blanket. If it was only a tiny match, she could douse it with a cup of water.

Let us imagine that a small fire started in the girl's kitchen. The fire could easily be put out, but the young girl wasn't sure how to do it exactly right. So she went outside and watered the roses, which she did know how to do exactly right. The fire kept getting bigger and bigger until the house burned down.

Meanwhile, the young girl did a very good job of watering the roses. She made sure that the leaves did not get too wet so that black spots would not grow on them. When the firefighters came to put out the remains of the fire in the burned-down house, they asked her why she watered the roses when the house was on fire. She said, "Because I know how to water the roses but am not sure how to put out fires."

Comment:

For many patients with eating disorders, especially anorexia nervosa, self-starvation is a practiced skill that can be turned to with satisfaction and perfection when any "fire" occurs in life. There is no situation that is so serious that it cannot be temporarily avoided by self-starvation. The art of losing weight is like the young girl's ability to water the roses—it can be done with great skill, but it is the wrong activity for the situation. Losing weight gives the illusion of control, of being able to do something perfectly, and quells the anxiety that comes when life is not so neat, or when troubling situations provoke fear. Maybe it is better to put out fires poorly than to water roses perfectly.

A similar analogy is that some activities make about as much sense as rearranging the deck chairs on the Titanic. Whatever the analogy, when houses are on fire, you either put the fire out or call for help.

Originally published in 1993.

2

The Catsup Bottle: Go All the Way

binge eating, bulimia, impulsivity

Let us imagine you are at a party and you are wearing your best dress. Whatever the style, it is just what you like. The color is perfect. You look good in it and feel confident. At the party, they are serving hamburgers, french fries, and salad. As you put some catsup on your hamburger, you spill a drop on your dress.

When you see what you have done, you start dumping the whole bottle all over the dress! After all, it's already dirty! Since you weren't able to keep yourself from getting a drop on the dress, you go all the way and finish the bottle. You dump some on the skirt; you dump some on the sleeves. There's a little left over; you pour some on your nose; you spill some on your shoes. After all, when you got a drop on your dress, you failed to stay completely clean. So you stop all this trying to be perfectly clean and get the rest of that catsup all over you!

What's wrong with this story? You think this is a silly story? Nobody in their right mind would do that! But isn't that what you do with your binge eating? If you have planned a healthy and balanced approach to eating, but you happen to eat some extra food, why do you go ahead and eat everything in sight? A slip in eating is not a moral failure or a knockout, no more than a drop of catsup on a skirt. Recognizing that you have started overeating does not mean you have to go on to binge.

Sure, there are some obvious differences. First, there is the pressure of hunger that builds up if you have been dieting. But there are also some sensible similarities. Why not think about them? You don't have to go to extremes. Maybe it has been hard trying to be so perfect or to be so worried about what others think.

Comment:

The approach of all-or-none behavior and reasoning generally doesn't make sense in real life. Once you recognize that a plan hasn't worked perfectly, it is sensible to make the rest of the plan work as well as possible instead of throwing it all away. Some people get the idea that because they get up on the wrong side of the bed, the whole day is ruined. It makes a lot more sense to interrupt any pattern of behavior or thinking that's not helpful or healthy as soon as it's recognized and get back on track right away, than to throw up your hands and go to the opposite extreme.

Sometimes this all-or-none reasoning comes from perfectionism, with the thought that if you're not perfect, you're a failure. Sometimes it comes from having excessively rigid or impossible standards that nobody can possibly keep, so you find relief in swinging in the opposite direction. Whatever the reason, the best approach to recognizing that eating is beginning to get out of control is to regain reasonable, moderate control, and then be kind to yourself.

The obvious, sensible thing to do when you spill a drop of catsup on your dress or suit is to go to the nearest water faucet and gently dab the area with cold water (or better, plain club soda) so that there will be a minimal stain, and then get back to enjoying the party.

Originally published in 1993.

3

The Indian and the Chessboard

recovery tool & all ED

Once upon a time, a long while ago, a poor Indian, not a Native American, but a real member of the wonderful subcontinent of India, did a noble deed to save the life of the ruling maharajah. In gratitude, the maharajah offered the poor Indian the choice of either half of his kingdom or anything else he wanted. The wise, but poor Indian declined the offer of half of the kingdom and said instead that he would prefer to have tomorrow, one grain of wheat on the first square of a chessboard and on the next day, two grains on the second square and so on until 64 days had passed. The maharajah thought this was a very modest request and granted it right away. So on the next day he received one grain of wheat, and on the second day, two grains of wheat, and on the third day, four grains of wheat, doubling the amount each day. What the maharajah didn't realize was that after 64 days the formerly poor Indian did not own half of his kingdom but owned his whole kingdom.

What I'd like you to do today is to make just one little step toward health. Tomorrow, I'd like you to make two steps. And then on the third day, to double that. Just keep doubling your efforts in a comfortable, natural, gradual way and soon you will own your own kingdom. Taking things a step at a time and aiming for progress, not perfection, will eventually give you much more than you can realize.

Comment

Sometimes the hardest thing in the therapy of a person with an obsessional temperament is getting her or him to take the first step. This is applicable for obesity, for overweight patients, as well as for a sensitive, avoidant anorexic or a discouraged bulimic. Taking the smallest step on the first day and following this up on the next day with a second step, and then twice that the third day will lead to freedom. (Whatever the fear, whatever the need, just start with one step at a time and keep doubling it.)

Originally published in 1993.

4

The Emperor Has No Clothes—Do You?

recovery tool, thinness & weight loss

You may have heard this story as you were growing up. Once upon a time there was an emperor who was very vain and proud of himself. He gathered around him many courtiers who liked to play on his vanity and take advantage of him. One day, the chief courtier said that an especially fine tailor was coming to town and would make the emperor a new set of clothes.

Soon this visiting tailor comes to town and measures the emperor for his new set of clothes. He then hurries off to make the clothes and comes back to present them to the emperor. All the court stands around and says "ooo" and "aaah" as the tailor brings out a nonexistent set of clothes. "HOW wonderful you look, emperor!" says one court flunkey. "You are now the best dressed emperor in the world," says another court member.

Soon the emperor leads a parade through town and all the people say to his majesty how beautifully he is dressed. In fact, he is stark staring naked, looking like a jaybird, showing a little gooseflesh whenever the wind blows. Finally, a little boy, who has not learned all the silly customs of the court and all the excess deference of the population, says, "Why doesn't the emperor have any clothes on?"

Your concern with losing weight and our society's concern with losing weight represents just this kind of mass delusion and hypocrisy. There is not the slightest evidence that losing weight below a healthy, normal range does you any good, and yet, people are going "ooo" and "aaah" over skinny models who look like fried chicken wings with bones sticking out and whose cheekbones look like they have come from a concentration camp. What an absurdity that we should be putting on parade people who look ill and admiring them. Everyone is afraid to say, "The emperor has no clothes." Everyone is afraid to say that losing weight is, in fact, a wasted effort. Just think about it—are you an emperor or empress walking around with no clothes, thinking how beautiful you look? Some little kid who has never read a fashion magazine, might just say that, in fact, you look ill and starved and hungry and thin and cold.

Comment

Our cultural emphasis on the value of thinness is absolutely astounding. To call it a delusion catches the right emotional note, but technically there is no delusion going on. It is a complex combination of an overvalued idea, a cultural more, a mass consensus, and brainwashing. Not only do few people say the emperor has no clothes, but those who do tend to be rejected. People don't like to be told the truth that they have, in fact, been taken in by a big lie.

Originally published in 1993.

5

The Stockholm Syndrome

family dynamics, people pleasing

Some time ago, as happens from time to time, a group of innocent citizens were taken hostage by terrorists. In order to keep themselves from being killed and maybe to get food, they started to agree more and more with their captors. The situation went so far that when finally the authorities came to release the hostages, these guileless prisoners started attacking the police and defending the terrorists.

Many people with eating disorders came from generally positive, functional families. Some do not. I've seen too many patients from difficult backgrounds to gloss over their stories.

When you were growing up, especially when it was a bad situation at home, you learned to survive by not disagreeing too much, by trying to please the people who imprisoned you, by pretending you thought the way they did; you appeared to adopt their values and ways. The problem is, when it came time to be released, you did not realize that this was just a temporary way to survive growing up and not a good way to live.

You told me your father was a bully, and that your mother took his side when he got abusive. Well, having agreed to confront them in our next family session, you now defend them and say they're not so bad after all. They didn't really mean it. Just think about what you've done—you've learned to protect yourself so thoroughly that finally, when you have a chance to begin over in a safe environment, you start making excuses for them.

Please understand that we plan to approach these issues in family sessions in a sensitive and experienced way. We don't even have to do it right now. Maybe it's something you want to do in your own way. But for goodness sake, recognize what you're doing when you start rewriting the past and saying that things weren't so bad after all. This is what Anna Freud called "identification with the aggressor"—a way of staying safe when you're growing up by identifying with bullies so that you don't get hurt or killed. Stop this pattern now that you have a chance to do things differently. What if this model leads you to bully your own children. Let's start now to recognize that that unhealthy way of surviving in the past is over, and begin a new pattern.

Comment

One phenomenon in psychiatry that is truly amazing is the defense mechanism of identification with the aggressor. Residents and psychology interns, who otherwise are pretty skeptical, think I'm psychic when I predict that a patient who has been abused by her parents will defend them as soon as I criticize them. Lo and behold, I am an advocate for the patient, and tell them that growing up in that household was a terrible experience, that their parents were truly unkind, unfair, and frankly abusive. (I *only* say this when there is good, objective evidence that this was the case.) Inevitably, the patient starts saying that I shouldn't say those mean things and, really, the parents weren't so bad. This could go for a mean teacher, a sadistic scoutmaster, a bullying aunt, or anybody in authority. It is interesting that in a family of several children, often only one child is abused, while the others get off relatively scot-free.

In this kind of abnormal setting, sometimes the person who tries hardest to please the parents and identifies most with them is, in fact, the person who may be most severely abused. Sometimes the openly defiant kid gets away with it, or the "magnolia blossom" child, who is totally weak, may also escape mistreatment. But the person who is perceived as having power is abused until she or he learns to survive by identifying with the aggressor.

How wonderful when an insightful patient working in therapy gets the concept of identification with the aggressor, recognizes that she or he has been perpetuating the pattern, and then starts changing how they relate to the former aggressor in an ultimately healthier manner. This might mean disengaging from the aggressor or standing up for oneself in a safe setting.

Originally published in 1993.

6

Let's Go to a County Fair

anorexia nervosa, anxiety, recovery tool

Imagine that you're at a good old-fashioned county fair. There are prizes for quilts, pies, pigs, and corn. Imagine you walk past the exhibits and games until you come to a pie-throwing exhibit. In this event, someone volunteers to raise money for a local charity by sitting behind a piece of fake scenery and sticking his or her head through a hole. People who come up and plunk down a dollar get the chance to throw a cream-filled pie at the unfortunate, but willing, victim.

Whether this is a kind or a cruel activity is another subject. The point is that worrying about the future feels like being the target in a pie-throwing game. Your head is way out there, in the future, getting all of the cream pies thrown at it. Your hands are behind the plywood scenery, unable to protect you.

Anticipatory anxiety gives you the worst of both worlds. It causes you to be fearful. Maybe it makes you want to return to your skinny, anorexic body weight to keep from ever having to face the future. Even when your anorexia improves, you may be left with anticipatory anxiety. Let's get your head out from in front of the pie throwing game and back into the present. The here and the now are the only place and the only time you can ever do anything about. Besides, getting out from behind that exhibit means you don't have to face those cream pies. Instead, you can use your hands to deal with other things that you face right now, things that are real and not part of a county fair game.

Comment

Patients with anorexia nervosa are prone to fearing the future. They project into it their worst fears, which come from imagination, bad personal experiences, family history and genetics, and from their anxious personality traits. Because all of these things are imagined happening in the future, there is no chance of doing anything about them in the present, so the result is a loss of the present as well as a painful fear of the future. It is a double loss. Sticking solidly in the here-and-now is the best way to deal with anticipatory anxiety. We need to keep heads and hands in the present where we can do something about what is going on.

Originally published in 1994.

7

The Long Bike Trip

anorexia nervosa, weight loss, hunger, exercise

Imagine that you went for a long, enjoyable bike trip on a hot summer day. You forgot your water canteen, and the water fountain you were expecting to drink from at the halfway point was broken. As you arrived home a couple of hours later, a friend meets you at your house and says, "Hurry, put your bike away. Let's go to a movie. There's a great new film at the Bijou." So off you go to see the latest thriller or romance. When you mention that you would like to stop for a drink of water, your friend says, "No, we have to go right now or we won't make the movie."

So there you are at the film. What are thinking about? The thriller diller? Who done it? Probably not. No matter what's doing on the screen, after that long, hot, dusty bike ride without a canteen and the water fountain broken, you're thinking about water. Why don't you say to yourself, "Just forget about thirst. Why bother with water when the movie's going on? Put it out of your mind and look at the screen." You know why. You can't put it out of your mind because you're thirsty.

Comment

Most people understand that when they are thirsty, the natural thing to do is to drink. But it is hard to convince people that hunger has a similar demanding quality on attention and behavior. Somehow, the idea has been promoted that we should be able to abstain from food, reduce our weight, and not have to deal with the resulting persistent, intrusive hunger.

Actually, stability of body weight and the driving force of hunger are much more ingrained in our biology than many people would like to believe. Hunger is a signal that the body is short on food energy. You can no more turn off your hunger than you can turn off your thirst. If you deny hunger, it sneaks out and organizes your activities in ways that you may not realize. Studies have shown that starved people think more about food than nonstarved people. They dream and fantasize about recipes, they read cookbooks, and get more involved with food. For anorexic patients, this often means preparing food for others to eat but not eating it themselves. It may lead to taking jobs in restaurants or fast-food chains.

Why this big surprise that when you're hungry, your mind will think about food and will direct your body's activities toward satisfying that need? We appear to deny the biology of hunger but endorse the biology of thirst. The only sensible approach to hunger is to accept it and to deal with it knowledgeably. This means eating regular, balanced meals, not dieting. Hunger is a signal from the "old brain" or limbic system crying out, "Give me a break, stop ignoring my needs!" Much of what we think of as anorexia nervosa is really the effect of starvation on our psychology, biology, and behaviors.

Originally published in 1994.

8

Pulling Weeds and Planting Flowers

all ED, therapy, health promotion

Let's imagine it is a nice spring day and you want to start a garden. You go out and see that there are a lot of weeds. You put on your old comfortable clothes and worn gardening gloves, kneel down, and start pulling out those weeds. Soon all those weeds are gone and you feel pleasantly tired but proud about what you've done. There's that old garden free of weeds, with the good dirt clearly visible again. So you take off your gloves, walk in the house, sit down, and tell yourself what a nice garden you have.

What's wrong with this picture? Of course, you say, you have to plant some flowers! Well, effective psychotherapy is more than pulling up weeds, and trying to get rid of the rocks and twigs that are covering up the good earth. It means also planting flowers (or trees, bushes, vegetables, you name it!). The whole purpose of removing your self-defeating patterns of behavior, recognizing what hasn't worked well, is to start cultivating thoughts and behaviors that produce "flowers." Getting rid of the problem areas is only the first step to growth and development. The real purpose of psychotherapy is to help you get on with your life, to produce something good and worthwhile, to grow flowers. Effective gardening does not stop after pulling out weeds. Interestingly, the old Greek word for peace, ειρήνη, does not mean only absence of war, it means a time of productivity, of fertility, of true tranquility.

Comment

Some physicians and psychologists consider promoting growth and developing health as a wasted effort. The most narrow concept of medicine is that it exists to treat disease. An equally important purpose of medicine, however, is more positive— to prevent disease and to promote growth—and, only when these efforts don't work, to identify and promptly treat disease.

Children don't need only the absence of noxious influences; they need the presence of healthy stimuli. Sometimes these healthy, growth-promoting influences can be pretty rough-and-tumble, and need not be like fancy health spas. They could be present in the family of a tenant farmer in Iowa, with only a couple of pigs and a few acres of corn, but with the whole family working together as a unit to feed themselves, and to have an occasional laugh on a Saturday night, telling stories, singing songs, and making homemade birthday gifts.

We should be at least as good at identifying the factors that go into promoting health, growth, and development, as we are in identifying and removing disease. Nature does not like a vacuum. Especially in psychological areas, taking away some symptoms without promoting growth can be ineffective. Perhaps that is why two of the most validated treatments for bulimia—cognitive-behavioral therapy and interpersonal psychotherapy—are effective. They deal with replacing unhealthy ways of thinking with healthy ways and improving distressed relationships. Clearing weeds without planting seeds or nurturing growth is creating a barren moonscape instead of a growing, productive, beautiful garden.

Originally published in 1994.

9

A Knight in Shining Armor

recovery tool, all ED, therapy, defense mechanism

Can you imagine those glorious days of the Middle Ages when knights went about fighting for the rights of distressed damsels and saving the world from bad people? As Margaret Mead reportedly said, "The good old days were basically pretty rotten." The Crusades were actually a nasty affair and ineffective for the Crusaders. Let us not now, however, discuss whether these knights were altruistic or misguided in their aims. Even if we take a slightly cynical view of history, there is something inspiring about imagining the storybook good knights who took care of the poor, the unfortunate, and the distressed, who rode into battle with lances outstretched as their horses charged forward to correct the wrongs of the world.

Can you imagine how silly it would be if a knight in shining armor were to go into combat today against foreign troops attacking our country? What chance would they have against missiles or tanks? Let us hope war doesn't come, but if it does, we need to be prepared to fight it with adequate up-to-date defenses, not with knights in shining armor.

The kind of psychological defenses you are using now were first used long ago in your personal history. For whatever the reason, you developed these defenses when you were growing up. What I'm asking you to do now is to discard the out-of-date armor and recognize that those old defenses are no longer adequate for your current situation. Your defenses aren't bad; they are simply ineffective for you in a more grown-up context.

There are some real-life stresses you need to deal with, including becoming healthy in weight, and letting go of binges and purges. An important part of your struggle to become well involves learning to deal with stress by using appropriate, effective, truly adult defenses to deal with the current world. For example, it is okay to postpone responding to someone who makes an uncomfortable comment until you have a chance to think through a response. You don't have to please others as long as you are true to your self. You can be assertive and disagree diplomatically with people who seem to hold all the power. Identify your outdated defenses, and use ways of coping that are up-to-date for today's world and who you are now.

Comment

Defense mechanisms characteristic of neurotic styles do not evolve from the wish to suffer, or to be ineffective, but because they were necessary and represented the only way to cope, considering the developmental stresses that were threatening. But out-of-date defenses can be death traps and can imperil people living in the modern world. Of course, getting rid of all old armor completely and not developing new armor may leave a person looking like a molting bird or a hermit crab outside its shell—defenseless

Originally published in 1994.

10

The Door and the Carpenter's Plane

anxiety, recovery tool, compulsivity

In our session last week we agreed that some change is essential for you. And now, this week, you're saying that you can never change your stripes, because you're a tiger and not a leopard. You're even a little bit angry, because you think that how I want you to be is impossible. Let's look again at the situation.

Let's imagine that you're going down into your carpenter's workroom, but the door is sticking. You look up and you see that the top of the door is stuck to the frame, so that every time you try to open the door you have to push it or pull it very hard. Now what is the solution to the problem? Do you have to get a brand new door? No. Instead, you take a carpenter's plane and shave down the top of the door to keep it from sticking. You only have to smooth it down a little bit.

Well, that's what I'm asking you to do in terms of the way you think and the way you behave in situations that cause you anxiety. I'm not suggesting that you stop going to work and become a beach bum. What I am suggesting is that you will become slightly less anxious at work, if you lighten up just a little bit and do things at a slightly more reasonable pace, instead of the way you usually push yourself. You don't need a new door, just shave it where it's sticking.

Let's look at the areas in your life where a small tweak might be helpful. Often, you don't have to change a lot to make things go much better.

Comment

Sometimes people misinterpret an agenda for change by getting angry or frightened and saying it is impossible to become completely different. Usually what helps most are small changes in critical areas to produce meaningful freedom instead of radical changes that would be artificial or unachievable for the patient. Change may sound more possible and realistic when you use the image of a plane shaving down a door that sticks. This is a metaphor that one of my friends uses often, and, in fact, he has several planes in his office to make his point.

Originally published in 1994.

11

Dr. Faustus and the Perfect Male Body

males, exercise, steroid abuse

You may have heard the story of the fellow who makes a pact with the devil to get a beautiful woman, fame, fortune, and lots of other goodies, but at the price, eventually, of his soul. The kind of pact that you have made by your plan to create a perfect body shape is pretty similar. The only difference is that in the end you may lose your body as well as your soul. Some of your friends at the gym told you that if you take steroids, you'll bulk up and win that weight-lifting prize at last. They promise you a 46-inch chest, ribs of steel, and thighs like oak trees. I know you've been disappointed the last two years when you haven't ranked in the top three at the body-building contest. But using steroids to get that title is not much different from what Dr. Faustus did: he sold the future for a short-term goal.

These drugs will rot your liver, shrink your testes, and give you "roid rage" as well as acne. They may promote cancer. A sound mind in a sound body is the real goal. You're going to get neither with steroids. Let's flush those steroids down to the Mutant Ninja Turtles. Real progress in body building through good lifting technique, cross-training, low-carb food, and rest between days at the gym will produce lasting results you can be proud of instead of fake results from a deal with the devil.

Comment

Many young male athletes say they would be willing to die in five years if only, at the present time, they could win an Olympic gold medal. Young people, especially young guys, often have a sense of invulnerability and no real concept of future consequences. Bulking up now is all that counts. This way of thinking and behaving may come partly from certain personality traits, but also from the age-old existential yearning for quick results by dangerous means. A burning intensity for a short-term goal may lead to loss of prudence and common sense and, in fact, to dangerous pacts with the devil of drugs.

It is possible that young males are predisposed, on a sociobiological basis, to this intensity of response in order to achieve quests or make threats, as part of an age-old survival mechanism. Thus, the quest for gratification may need to be redirected and guided rather than quashed. Asking young males to think through and decide whether the end justifies the means may sound old-fashioned and unexciting, but in the end, looking skeptically at these pacts will lead to a longer and more satisfying life. If only the prefrontal cortex could be connected to the limibic system securely by the age of 15 instead of 25!

Originally published in 1994.

12

The Miner's Lamp

recovery tool, anxiety, avoidant personality

Let's imagine that you're working in a deep, dark West Virginia coal mine. You've pretty well cleaned out the area of coal you can see with the miner's lamp mounted on top of your helmet. Of course, it only lights up the area right in front of you, but what if you need to dig further into the vein of coal? You have to step forward in the darkness before you can see what lies ahead. That's the way it is with a lot of life. Many times we're in situations where things are dark around us and we have only a miner's lamp to see with. We may not be able to see any further until we take a step into the darkness. But, lo and behold, as you step forward into the darkness, the darkness turns to light!

You have some avoidant features in your personality, which means that, among other things, you're usually anxious about what's coming up. You worry when you can't know absolutely what will happen. But if you put together all the facts you do know, you'll see everything will work out all right. Really, it's probably not going to be all that dangerous to go to the job interview, bowling league next Friday, or family birthday party. Don't fret over the darkness. Think about the idea that you can only see what will come next when you step into it and light the way.

Comment

Fearful anticipation of dangers unforeseen may be behind the inhibited action of patients with avoidant personality disorder. Many individuals will not move unless they can see everything ahead of them completely clearly, and be 100% assured that everything is safe. Well, nobody can completely assure any of us that when we get out of bed in the morning we won't slip on a banana peel. We have to use our common sense and work with the probabilities, not the feared possibilities. Staying in bed, after all, is dangerous and can produce pulmonary emboli, loss of calcium in the bones, and other problems. I'm not suggesting here that we encourage a person to dive into dark and murky waters or to walk off a cliff without looking. We're talking about helping people who are excessively inhibited to experiment with taking reasonable, small risks, despite their fears of the unknown (e.g., being hurt, rejection, not being 100% successful).

Sometimes the simple story of a miner's lamp that shows light further ahead only when you step ahead gets across the idea that action may not be as dangerous as some think it is. In fact, a step ahead may be essential. So, let's suggest to people with avoidant personalities that, once they've made a reasonable survey of the objective dangers of a situation compared to possible benefits, they should take the forward step.

Originally published in 1994.

13

Watch Your Side of the Road: Here I Come

body image, therapy, perceptual distortion

You just told me you feel so very fat even though your experienced counselor says you are still medically underweight. Could we put that issue aside while I tell you a story? In the meantime, may I ask you to hold my glasses for a minute? By the way, without my glasses, I can't see the large writing on the poster behind you any longer. How would you react if I were to get behind the wheel of an automobile now and start driving on the highway without my glasses? You're absolutely right! You would stay off the road.

My glasses are necessary to correct my vision. In a way, we have a similar problem, but I know I need glasses to correct my vision. I would like you to think about the idea that you also have a problem in accurate perception—not perception of the road, but concerning your body size and shape. Unfortunately, there is no optical shop to get a pair of glasses that we can prescribe for these kinds of misperceptions. Instead, I would like your healthy self to accept the fact that you do have a problem in accurately perceiving your body size and shape. We don't understand this kind of perception difficulty as well as my nearsightedness. It is not a matter of will power or a personal failing. In fact, it's a bit of a mystery.

We know that if you will trust us to work with you, you can learn to accurately "see" yourself in a realistic, objective, but loving way. Let's work together to find a mental prescription for the kind of eyeglasses you need, so you can get on the highway of your life without crashing. Driving on the highway of life in our society requires accurate vision regarding your body size.

Comment

Perceptual distortion is found in many eating-disordered patients. It is an imprecise phenomenon, not absolutely pathognomonic, but common and consequential. A number of studies have found that outcome after treatment is highly correlated with the degree of persisting perceptual distortion. Many of the abnormal eating disorder behaviors are driven by perceptual distortion.

The technical methods to measure perceptual distortion are varied. They began with Russell and Slade's test of moving two points of light in a dark room until various body widths were estimated by the patient. Other recent methods have included lens distortion, the circle-a-figure test, and a simple string test, whereby patients estimate on a string the width of their waist, hips, etc.

Hilde Bruch led the way in the understanding of eating disorders in our society. She made major contributions from a developmental and psychodynamic, but not specifically psychoanalytic, perspective. One of her few technical errors, in retrospect, was to use the phrase "perceptual distortion of delusional proportion." The perceptual distortion of these patients remains an enigma. It is shared by the formally obese, sometimes present in pregnancy, and those who have had limbs amputated. It is not, however, a delusion in any way. Patients will readily say that they understand they are excessively thin from a medical perspective, but they still "feel" fat. They suffer from a cognitive misperception, but this is a distortion of perceptual cues, not a fixed, false belief, as in a psychosis.

Just as the understanding of this phenomenon is imprecise, so treatment is not completely agreed upon. But whatever methods are used, taking into account perceptual distortion and attempting to help patients develop a more accurate body image in a loving but objective way are integral parts of the treatment of eating disorders.

Originally published in 1994.

14

Will the Real Parents Please Stand Up?

reverse parenting, family dynamics

Let's imagine that your mom and dad are in bed. They're wearing their pajama sleepers-you know, those long jammies that have feet in them like babies wear. Then let's imagine you, as a toddler, putting on grown-up shoes with high heels that you only half fit into. You're wearing a long dress that comes down below your ankles and drags behind you. Finally, let's imagine that you're bringing milk and cookies to your parents in bed. They're saying that they've had a hard day, and you're responding, "That's OK, this will make you feel better." And the funny thing is, everybody acts as if this is normal. What's wrong?

You've grown up in an untypical household, where you've had to be a parent to your parents. The little scene that I've just sketched for you mentally is no more silly than the situation you've gone through from the time you were young. For whatever the reason, the facts are that your mom and dad were not well suited to be married to each other or be parents. Their negative behavior and emotional issues of their own made them incapable of properly caring for a child.

Somehow, you got the idea that you both caused the bad feelings and are responsible for fixing them, that it's your mission to make your parents feel good. When you should have been a kid learning to play, you learned, instead, to be a little caregiver. The sad thing is that you were not equipped for the role, yet you had to carry it out. No one told you that it wasn't fair or it would never work. But you perceived from your folks that you were responsible for their problems and had to make them better. But you were too young to protect yourself, or to protest.

We have a real challenge ahead of us—for you to learn how to play, to go through the stages that you missed, and to look forward to being an adult, not the kind of fake adult, parent role you saw at home, but a life where it is okay to have feelings, and to say no, and to make your own choices.

Comment

The phenomenon of "reverse parenting" is very real in some families. I've seen patients with eating disorders who carried the burden of being the parents' caretaker. There can be harmful consequences from a combination of immature, needy, narcissistic, and callous mother or father and a vulnerable child, who is both sensitive to parental moods and behaviors and thinks that he or she is the reason for the parents' problems. Illogically, these kids often do a reasonably good job at this reverse parenting, so this facade and parody of real parenting is maintained. This dichotomy can turn a kid off from wanting to be an adult, yet makes them scared of going back to being a kid.

Originally published in 1995.

15

The Sinking of the Titanic

anorexia nervosa, compulsivity, denial

Do you remember the story of the Titanic—the classy passenger liner that proudly steamed from Europe to New York back in 1912, giving great assurance to everyone on board that it was the most modern passenger liner ever built and could take care of any problem along the way, like icebergs? Tragically, the great ocean liner struck an iceberg and its belief of being invulnerable didn't hold water, but that's another story.

Imagine that you and your family are on the Titanic, as many families were. Imagine the ship starting to take on water and beginning to sink. What do you do? You start rearranging the deck chairs. They are not quite in order. The colors aren't lined up. As this great ocean liner is sinking, you are fussing with the nice deck chairs, making sure everything is in order. You are very good at it, but what's the point?

In some ways, what you are doing with your nutritional intake is rearranging the peas and carrots while the ship (your life) is going down. You have made it clear that everything is going just fine: you are having a few more peas and two bites of chicken, instead of only one. In fact, what you are doing is rearranging the deck chairs while the Titanic is going down.

THE SINKING OF THE TITANIC

The purpose in telling you this story is to get you to stop rearranging the deck chairs. Instead, take the helm of the ship and see if you can't get it upright again. If that doesn't work, you can put out a distress signal on your transmitter. If that doesn't work, you can find the lifeboat. The point is, the first thing you need to do is stop rearranging the deck chairs and think about your safety. We don't want you to lose hope and jump off the ship. We want you to take effective action to do something, because the situation is desperate. Rearranging the food on your plate, pretending you're eating a bit more, won't work.

Comment

The denial of extreme thinness and the illusion of taking action in the face of obvious lack of improvement are extraordinary events I see time and time again. To have an emaciated patient glare at me with the kind of angry intensity that would have gotten her an Oscar is amazing. I am told that things are just fine—and why aren't I giving her more credit—because it's clear she's trying the best she can, and she had more vegetables last night than she has ever had. Doctors can get caught in this "Chamberlain at Munich" kind of agreement. One adolescent psychiatrist called me and asked to discuss a patient. He said that after months of intense negotiation and sincere and energetic good-willed therapy with this young woman, they had finally agreed that the patient's weight would not go below a certain low number. It was a firm, solid agreement, and didn't I think that this was healthy? I said it was just about as healthy as putting a lock on a house after all its contents had been stolen.

Ibsen said, "Rob the average man of his life-illusion, and you rob him of his happiness." There is something very rude in confronting starved patients with the folly of their little nutritional rearrangements when their body is getting thinner and weaker. But it has to be done. They need to be confronted, kindly, about their illness. Sometimes a provocative story makes the point better than dialogue alone. They certainly know what I am saying when I suggest to them they are rearranging the deck chairs on the Titanic. That phase is one that my friend David Edwin uses often, and I have always appreciated the drama of ineffective but expert activity while the ship sinks.

Originally published in 1995.

16

What Does the Tombstone Say?

anorexia nervosa, thinness, quality of life

Have you ever gone for a walk in the country and come across a church-yard? Or maybe you've visited New Orleans and looked at some of the tombstones there. If someone has died recently in your family, this is a sensitive subject. But if that hasn't happened and you are just visiting a historical place, it is interesting to wander and look at what these tomb-stones say. Many tourists when visiting the Capital go to the monuments for Washington, Lincoln, Jefferson, and others.

Let's use your imagination and say that 200 years from now people are walking through a country churchyard, or a big city cemetery, or wherever your tombstone is. They approach and read it. What will they read? If you continue pursuing thinness as extremely as you are now, it's possible the dates will show a short time between when you were born and when you'll die. That's not meant to scare you: it's reality. What I wonder, however, is what will the epitaph say? "This person spent all of her life trying to be thinner." Or perhaps: "Here died a really skinny girl who did nothing else."

It's serious business, and maybe too serious for the moment, but think about what's going to happen in the future. If you're familiar with

A Christmas Carol by Dickens, you know that a personal look into the future can be a very effective way to change your life. As Scrooge looked into the future at an empty life where people were glad to get rid of him, he changed how he lived. Try it out on yourself. See what you would like your tombstone to say, or how you would like your obituary in the newspaper to read. Do you really want it to say you spent all your life worrying about weight?

Comment

The challenge of the existential aspect of eating disorders is often neglected. Coming to terms with issues of meaning and suffering is usually part of a long-term psychotherapy program. Sometimes it helps to challenge a starved eating-disordered person's sense of invulnerability by asking her or him to imagine themself (as the ghost in the Charles Dickens story did with Scrooge) as being a lot older, maybe deceased, and what people in the future would say about them. The purpose of this effort is not to be unnecessarily gloomy, but to challenge the anorexic person to live here and now so that they will have created a life worthy of living and worth looking back on, with more to say than: "I was thin."

Originally published in 1995.

17

Your Day in Court: Two Endings

thinness, weight obsession, recovery tool

Sometimes, mystery stories and films have more than one possible ending. Let's imagine you're called to court to face a serious charge; and, there are two different endings to the story.

Basic Story

One evening, while you are at home relaxing, drinking a diet soda, and wearing an extra sweater around you to keep warm, there is a sudden, hard knock on the door. With a certain amount of anxiety and a rapid heartbeat, you go to open the door. Two armed police officers hand you a summons to court saying you must appear tomorrow morning to face serious charges, which will be revealed when you receive your sentence from the judge.

After a restless night in bed, you gather your courage, dress in your best business clothing, and head for the courtroom. As you enter the court, people are shaking their heads and looking very sad for you (because of what you will have to face). You enter the main courtroom. The judge's bench is hidden by a curtain. So is the jury box.

The bailiff tells you that other, less serious charges such as murder, robbery, and kidnapping are heard in the side courts. Only the most serious crimes are reserved for this central court.

The bailiff then summons you to the front of the court and reads the indictment, "You have been accused of becoming fat, of developing cellulite in your thunder thighs, of having broken the first law of our society—to stay thin. Your jelly belly is a disgrace to our nation and an affront to public morals. You have failed society, your family, and your peers by committing this felony. How do you plead?"

You answer, "I did my best, I skipped breakfast and had only a salad for lunch. I couldn't help the binges in the evening when my aunt pressured me to have her homemade fried chicken and apple pie. I just couldn't say no. I realize I failed, but I plead not guilty with an excuse."

The bailiff asks if there are any other witnesses? Your girlfriends appear and say that yes, you did indulge shamefully. Your mother says that she tried to raise you right, but you ignored the diet camp doctor's advice and all the warnings on the refrigerator door.

The bailiff walks with you over to the jury as the curtain in front of the jury panel is removed. You are asked to address the jury, which consists of 12 members: the first six chairs have copies of *Glamour, Vogue, Elle, Seventeen,* the latest best seller, *Be Slender Today,* and a recorded version of "How to Defeat Your Appetite." In the last six chairs are four dresses and two suits, respectively, sizes 4, 3, 2, 1, 1/2, and 0.

You say to the jury, "I realize that I have failed you all and I ask for your mercy."

The bailiff commands, "Come before the judge."

The curtain is pulled away, and there the judge stands: A large white clinical scale with the word JUDGE printed on the metal indicator. The bailiff says: "Please step up to the JUDGE." You step up, stand on the scale, look down shocked, and step back, head and eyes lowered.

Ending 1

The bailiff reads the verdict as handed to her by the size 1/2 dress, who served as the foreperson of the jury. "You have been found to be piggish, self-indulgent, weak-willed, and fat. Guilty without excuse!"

The bailiff says, "The judge is too shocked to speak. I have been instructed to read the following sentence to you. You will receive 20 years of hard labor, with 10 miles of jogging required daily, no matter how cold the temperature or how ill you are. You will reject any foods before 3:00 PM, and after that, limit yourself to 500 calories a day. Your total fat intake must be less than 8 grams a day. You will not attend any parties or festivities associated with food. You will not receive the wafer at Mass because it is filled with calories. You will judge yourself as unworthy compared to the elegant members of the jury. If, after 20 years, you show more prominent ribs, and your thighs never touch, and you are truly sorry for your indulgence, you will be released to a parole of 800 calories a day."

Ending 2

Wait a minute, you say, "This is just a bad dream. The jury is rigged with the sickest objects in our society. I must have actually eaten that spicy chili, or gotten a touch of the flu, to have dreamed such a crazy dream where I would let these sick things judge me. And as for you, Mr. Judge you are nothing but a piece of metal that I have given my power to. You have no right to judge or sentence me, nor to spoil my day. I take back all the power I have given you and instead will live moderately today, seeking reasonable pleasure each day, looking for progress not perfection, and letting my well-regulated appetite and satiety guide me to eat until I feel comfortably full. I will exercise moderately when it is reasonable to do so, but will knock it off when it makes sense to stop. You are fired, Judge."

Comment

'Nuff said. Trusting yourself, be skeptical of sociocultural fads, and look for a reasonable balance between responsibility and pleasure, work and play, and your own needs and those around you. Pleasant dreams.

Originally published in 1995.

18

Playing to the Audience

people pleasing, recovery tool

Have you ever been in a school play? Most of us have taken part in a holiday play, or pageant, or school presentation. Let's imagine that you're set for a serious career as an actor or an actress. Here you are, having trained for many years, finally ready to make it on stage. It is opening night and the curtain goes up. You are acting in classical style as Juliet in Shakespeare's *Romeo and Juliet*. The audience loves what you're doing and they are applauding. Suddenly, you hear another group of people saying, "We don't like Shakespeare. We want you to do *My Fair Lady*." You look around and there is another curtain behind you that's gone up, with a different audience booing you as you declaim Juliet's great soliloquy: "Romeo, Romeo, wherefore art thou?" So you turn around and start doing *My Fair Lady*, humming a few bars and looking like Liza Doolittle. Just as you're getting out of breath, but finally satisfied that you have given this other audience what they want, you make a quarter circle turn and see a third audience saying, no they don't want either Shakespeare or *My Fair Lady*. They want you to perform the play on which the musical was based, *Pygmalion* by George Bernard Shaw.

Curtain down! What is going on here? Well, it's the same thing that is going on in your life. You are trying to play to too many different audiences. Whatever one audience wants, the other doesn't want. You see what an exhausting business this would be, playing to two, three, four, half a dozen audiences, all the time. The term we use for this tendency is "external locus of control." What that means is, you're always playing the role in life that the audience cheering most loudly around you wants. But, audiences are fickle. Mom might want one thing and Dad another. One friend could demand one action but your cousin another. Unless you start deciding what *you* want for yourself, and recognize that whatever you do is not going to satisfy everybody all the time, you'll be like this poor, tired actress playing to ever-changing audiences.

It's okay that not everybody likes what you do all the time. The question is: Do you like it? Have you decided what you'd like your play to be about? What role do you want to play? Your life is not a dress rehearsal. Choose your part and act it with confidence, now.

Comment

The concept of an external locus of control is like many useful psychiatric concepts—imprecise, not fully scientific, but very useful. Many of our eating disorders patients suffer from this style of interacting with the external world. Developmentally, it indicates a lack of "object constancy" and an attempt to please a variety of real or imagined external sources of nurturance and approval. Perhaps this is part of an inborn trait of personality and built into the nervous system, or perhaps it's something that's learned, or more likely some of both. Whichever it is, life is almost impossible to live when a person needs approval from ever-changing audiences on the outside, or from a variety of internalized demanding, non-nurturing objects.

Originally published in 1995.

19

Packing and Unpacking: When Will It End?

perfectionism, compulsivity, defense mechanism

Let's imagine that you have a favorite Aunt Tillie and her birthday is coming up. You've gone to the store and bought some wrapping paper. You're very excited about wrapping her gift and topping it off with a big beautiful bow. But then you look at it, and say, "NO, I should have used the other wrapping paper." So, you unwrap the package and go back to the store to buy the wrapping paper that you didn't get before. Now you are certain you have just the right one. You're excited about finally getting the perfect paper. Lo and behold, after you've wrapped the gift again, you are still not sure it's right. You really should have used the first paper, so you unwrap and rewrap the gift again. But, of course, when that's been done, and again topped with another bow, you can't stand it. You are absolutely sure that the second one was the right one, and so on, and so on, and so on.

You can imagine how frustrating this process would be. But that's what you are doing in your life. Anna Freud called this process "doing and undoing." She suggested that this process was a central theme in the lives of people who have obsessive-compulsive traits. It's very frustrating to make a choice and then to undo it and then to undo that choice. It's natural to wonder sometimes whether we have made the right decision. If we worry too much about the decision-making process, we can become paralyzed. Sometimes getting stuck is a symptom of depressive illness; sometimes it reflects a personality trait; sometimes it is a way of avoiding hurt. Doing and undoing is called a "defense mechanism." Defense mechanism means just that—a way to defend ourselves against anxiety about something bad that may happen if you don't do things in the right way.

Other analogies of doing and undoing come to mind, like driving down a road and not knowing whether to go left or right around an obstacle in the road. In the end, it may not make a big difference whether you go right or left as long as you go around the obstacle. Sometimes in life, when the best direction to take isn't obvious, it may not be very important whether you go right or left. Simply getting on and moving ahead may be more important than which direction you choose. Choosing the exactly correct dress to wear to a party, the perfect title for an essay at school, the most convincing phrase to use with a parent to gain approval—these are all like the wrapping and unwrapping business. Sometimes the decision itself is not as important as simply getting on with things. Perhaps the worry about being hurt is the real issue, or wanting to please others, or wanting never to make mistakes. Think about it—are you wrapping and unwrapping, writing and then deleting, going first right and then left? How about just getting on with it?

Comment

"Doing and undoing" is such a common defense that we may forget how frustrating it is to be living out that mechanism when it is present to a severe degree. By expressing our understanding through everyday examples, the meaning of this defense mechanism may be clearer, and we may appear more empathetic than when we use jargon words. The worries about making perfect choices, displeasing others, and being dominated by fear may all contribute to paralyzed decision making. Identifying what the fear is that lies behind the "doing and undoing" may be the first step to appropriate risk taking and to getting on with living life.

Originally published in 1995.

20

Plowing a Straight Line

recovery tool, all ED

Once, long ago, two farmers (cousins, in fact) owned farms side by side. In late March, when the ground finally started to soften, they decided it was time to start plowing. By tradition, the first farmer started on the west side of his long, narrow plot of ground, and the second farmer started on the east side of his long, narrow plot of ground. They agreed that by the end of the day they would treat themselves to a rest and refreshments at the Inn, which was situated directly in between their two narrow properties.

Both farmers hitched their plows to horses. The first farmer looked ahead at the Inn and kept his eye on it while he plowed. This was not easy, because he encountered many obstacles. Along the way, first he hit a large boulder and had to maneuver the plow around the rock, but he kept his eye on the Inn all the time. He then came to a rapidly running stream. Crossing the stream would mean getting his feet wet and muddy, and maybe even being carried away in the spring thaw, but he kept his eye on the Inn and walked swiftly across, counteracting the pull of the current, until he got to the other side. After making some further progress, he hit upon a hard patch of earth that was still frozen.

He had to work very hard to make a furrow through the hard frosted ground, but he kept looking ahead while he slowly nudged the plow along. After a while, his feet became entangled in vines that almost trapped him in that spot. He slowly but firmly picked up each foot and placed it ahead, sliding it in and out of the tangle while using the blade of the plow to slice through the vines.

For a while he lost sight of the Inn because of a fog that descended. Whenever the fog lifted, he looked ahead and reoriented the plow toward the Inn, but from time to time he couldn't see it. Finally, as he was getting closer to the Inn, he became very tired and almost gave up, but he kept his eyes on the light of the Inn and thought about how much more comfortable he would be once he got there. He finally arrived! When he entered, he put up his feet by the fireplace and ordered a large steaming bowl of soup and a big glass of water. He swapped stories with his friends and soon realized how worthwhile it was to keep his eye on the Inn.

The second farmer started at the other end, and he too gazed at the distant Inn. But he got distracted when he came to a large rock. At first he got angry and then became discouraged and thought the rock was too hard and too large. Instead of going around either side of the rock, he could not decide which way to go. He spent a long time waiting, until the horse pulled so hard that it pulled the plow over the rock. The stream also meandered through his property, and when he reached its edge, he worried about getting his feet wet and cold or being carried away by the stream. He waited there several weeks until the stream slowed to a trickle, but he had almost nothing to eat during this time except some water.

Later on, he came encountered a frozen, hard patch and while he waited another few weeks for the sun to soften the earth, he became very thin. When fog came, he was confused and frightened and did not know which direction to go, even after the fog lifted. Finally, entangled in vines and barely able to move, he became so tired and hungry that he thought he could not make it. He sat down for a long while. He was facing away from the Inn. When he turned around and caught sight of it, he realized he was farther away than when he had started. He decided the Inn must not be a very good place. It might be a mirage or an illusion. Perhaps the lights from the Inn were set up to fool people. You never knew what dangers might be present at an Inn that you had not visited before.

Comment

Getting well from an eating disorder is like taking a long journey to an Inn. The path to recovery is a lot like plowing a long furrow on land with unexpected obstacles. The Inn, of course, is the destination— a warm, comfortable place with adequate sustenance, social contact, and a sense of achievement. The large rock symbolizes many snags— seemingly hard, impossible to slice through, but possible to go around or over. The stream is the current of social pressure that easily pushes people off balance, pulling them downstream into the waterfall of self-starvation.

The hard patches represent times of plateau and seeming lack of further progress. When hard patches occur, farmers can either go slowly but steadily, keeping their eye on the Inn, or wait for weather conditions to become perfect. The vines represent all the nuisances and traps of detail. They seem powerful, but in fact they are all individual strands, which, once cut through, offer no lasting hold.

The fog that descends represents the loss of vision that may come from external circumstances or clouding of inner purpose. If the Inn can be visualized with the mind's eye, even when the physical eye does not see it, a farmer will not be far off course when the fog does lift, as it will. Even intermittent visions of the Inn serve to orient the direction of the plow. Tiredness represents discouragement and the fact that plowing a furrow or moving along the road to recovery takes hard work.

Once the Inn is reached, however, it is clear that the work was worthwhile. The Inn represents the reasonable expectation for a healthy, satisfying life. Only trust, hope, and education will allow a person to keep his or her eyes on the Inn and not dismiss it as a mirage or a deception until, finally, the Inn is a reality and not a vision.

Which kind of farmer are you?

Originally published in 1996.

21

Caught on Film: The Thief and the Pusher

all ED, internal pressures, compulsivity

Shasta was a modern-day heroine. Here's how it happened. Shasta had come from a broken family in the Ozarks. It was a tough family to live in, because whatever she did wasn't good enough. One day, while working as a waitress at the local coffee shop, she brought a cup of steaming coffee to a hiker who had taken a year off from college to think over his life. She quickly saw that he was different from the boys she had been raised with, and, they made plans to meet for pizza and a movie.

Things went along well and soon they were married. Her family was not at all pleased about her choice, but Shasta persisted and went off with Carl to his home in Pennsylvania. Shasta was very happy.

Shasta was energetic and eager to find a job. She convinced the local bank manager that she would make an excellent beginning teller and soon was promoted to local head teller, even though she had finished high school by correspondence. One day, while she was working at the drive-up window, a man wearing a ski cap jumped out of the car, pulled a gun, and demanded all the money in her register. She acted polite. calm, but a little dumb. She said she could not hear him. In a rage, he pulled off the mask and shouted, "I want all your money." She told him that she would wrap it up and hand it over, but please don't shoot because she did not want to get hurt. While she asked him questions to delay handing the money over, such as, "Would you like me to separate the bills into denominations," she was really reaching with her foot for the silent alarm to call the police.

When the police came, the thief had fled. Matching Shasta's description of the car, they found it abandoned in a shopping mall. Shasta told the police how she had tricked him into taking off his ski mask. As the police reviewed the security footage with Shasta's help, they came to a clear picture of the thief, then froze the picture on that frame, showing him in detail. He had a scar on one cheek and a distinctive tattoo on the hand that was holding the gun. When several suspects in a recent rash of bank robberies were brought into the police lineup later that week, Shasta identified the thief confidently and he was convicted.

Shasta was a heroine, but her moment of glory was marred by someone who kept pushing her. At least the thief was on the other side of the window, but this "pusher" kept pressing her from behind, making her feel she had to walk faster. She felt the pressure between her shoulder blades. Sometimes she thought she felt the pusher breathing down her neck. When she tried to finish one task, she felt the push toward an uncompleted task on the other side of her teller window. Even when she was walking home from work, trying to relax, she felt the push into a store to buy something that had been on her list.

Shasta thought, I was able to freeze-frame the thief on camera, maybe I can also catch this pusher the same way. He or she had been giving her these nudges in various places and at various times, but most often at work, where it seemed she would be pushed from job to job. She thought she might be able to capture this person (who was very subtle and not to be found when she turned around to see who was there) on the same camera that identified the thief. So, one day when she was working at counting her daily receipts and feeling a push toward the other side, where she had a number of late-night deposits to count, she positioned herself to the camera to get close-up details of this mysterious person. She did not turn around to see who it was, because she did not want to scare them away.

With the same ingenuity that challenged her to get this far in life, finally, she would find out who was making her life miserable. She studied the video moving it slowly frame by frame until she saw a hand placed right on her mid-back. She then zoomed in, showing more features, until she could identify this pusher, who had made life so difficult for her. It was very strange, however, because she could see an arm but no face. When she looked more closely, she was even more shocked than when the thief had pulled the gun. The hand pushing her was her own.

Comment

Many of our patients are caught in the trap of being able to deal with external challenges but not with internal pressures. They may have a relentless sense of compulsivity, with an attention to detail, but seem to be out of breath from all their perceived requirements. They are tired of the pressure. It never ceases, but they are unable to resist. I sometimes suggest to a patient who feels constantly pushed that we imagine a camera in our minds and look at it frame by frame. As we hold up this imaginary picture in the air, 1 tell them they have found the person pushing them relentlessly. I'm shocked to discover the identity—the arm pushing the patient is connected to the patient's shoulder.

Many patients externalize what are, in fact, internal forces, blaming the environment for what is a self-directed—although misdirected—intensity of effort. Since so much of their approval has to be externally generated, they take a while to realize that their relentless activity, sense of pressure, fear of stopping, and breathlessness toward tasks come from pressures they are applying to themselves. We sometimes do another imaginary exercise of reaching behind, taking that hand from the back and putting it in front while practicing relaxation. We imagine a reconnection of that arm to the shoulder, but with the hand in front, where it can reach for goals, instead of behind, where the pushing is relentless, secretive, and unwanted.

Originally published in 1996.

22

Landmines in Vietnam

family dynamics, conditioned responses, people pleasing

You may not be old enough to remember the war in Vietnam, but imagine the situation during that war (or any contemporary war). Soldiers often faced very difficult fighting conditions. They had to walk across fields and swamps where landmines might explode at any time. They might suddenly be killed, have a foot blown off, or find a spear or a poison dart thrust into them. Imagine how you would act if you had spent days, weeks, or months avoiding landmines. You wouldn't be surprised that a veteran walking down the street stateside would duck for cover whenever a car backfired. You wouldn't be surprised that they walk cautiously when they don't know what the terrain is like.

Unfortunately, if you've grown up in a calamitous family setting, you've also learned to avoid certain kinds of "landmines." Without having done anything wrong, you had to protect yourself from unexpected attack. You knew not to say anything to Dad if he was in a bad mood, because that might set him off. You avoided topics with Mom, because you knew she'd fly off the handle. It's not surprising that you're so cautious in relationships or taking risks.

But the fact is that you're out of landmine territory here. This means going comfortably into the family session and not worrying that somebody may blow up. Try to stop being so careful to censor your speech, or to be vague so that nobody disagrees with you. It's hard to change these conditioned emotional responses, but I'd like to help you walk confidently and stop acting as if there are still landmines ahead. Remember, you're only responsible for how you act and for what you say, not for how others respond. That's their choice.

Comment

Conditioned emotional responses represent a fundamental behavioral process meant for survival and for efficiency in daily life. When the normal conditioning process is distorted by learning to be excessively fearful and to practice avoidance behaviors during the years of development, this pattern may become lifelong, even when maladaptive. As a goal, let's work on deconditioning ourselves from the overgeneralized fear that landmines are everywhere.

Originally published in 1996.

23

Moth to the Flame

self-harm, impulsivity

This story is based on a conversation I had with my children.

"Do you remember when we were camping around Lake Coeur d'Alene? What a beautiful lake—deep, intensely blue, surrounded by pines on the hillsides. The French settlers who named it knew they had found one of the most beautiful lakes in America. Last summer, when we were visiting Aunt Lee and Uncle Tim, we all gathered together at a campfire on the edge of the lake the night before we had to leave. The same old stories seemed funnier than ever. When the campfire was blazing high, those marshmallows that we used to make s'mores never tasted better.

"Do you remember how we were sitting on the logs around the fire and saying, 'Look at those moths-those dumb moths. They keep getting so close to the flames, they get their wings singed and fall in the fire. Why doesn't someone tell them they're getting too close to the flame?' Do you remember that we went up to the campsite and lit the kerosene lantern with the old-fashioned glass chimney? The moths up around the campsite didn't seem to be any smarter than those down by the lake. They would circle around the kerosene light, coming closer and closer, until finally they got so close they were burned to a crisp.

"I was thinking the other day, kids, that people are a lot like those moths who get too close to the flame. Only human beings are supposed to be a lot smarter than moths—they should know that flying into the flame is a disaster. Do you remember the way Suzie's dad kept getting arrested for driving drunk, and finally lost his whole family? Then there was Joanie last year. She kept taking hits of cocaine, being sure she would never get dependent, and eventually she lost her job, boyfriend, and scholarship."

"Hey, Dad, that reminds me of Molly," my daughter said. "How could she keep going back to that boyfriend who kept beating her up? I don't understand it. She knew it would happen. She knew he was lying when he said he wouldn't hit her. Even before her bruises had healed, she told the police to drop the charges, and then went right back to him. Now she's got a broken arm, and an eye that may never get better."

"You're right," replied my son, "Human beings are not a whole lot smarter than moths sometimes. My French teacher went bankrupt last year from gambling at the riverboats in Davenport. She tried Gamblers Anonymous and an antidepressant that keeps you from acting on your compulsions. But she missed the gambling so much she stopped her medicine and went back to the casinos. I can't believe it—she's now left town and moved to Las Vegas."

Comment

As clinicians, we see people, time and time again, who act like moths drawn to the flame. Their left brain knows it doesn't make sense—they'll be hurt, they'll suffer in certain predictable ways—but they go right back, time and time again, to the same self-destructive situation. There are lots of theories about why people self-destruct. Very seldom is it from lack of knowledge. The new genetic discovery of a gene related to excitement seeking may have something to do with it. For some people, the immediate need, whether it's for relief of pain or for excitement, can be so strong that any sense of long-term consequences is overridden. I'm sure you've had the same sinking feeling I have, as a therapist, when you work to keep someone from self-destructing. These patients know what works and what doesn't work, and they go right back to what doesn't work. There's got to be something more than a single gene involved. Women who go back to abusive men, people who have addictions of different kinds, people who pull defeat from the jaws of victory—they do not act from lack of knowledge. We need to use consequences or boundaries to keep people from killing themselves, but in most situations they have to learn the hard way, and some never do.

Perhaps protecting people for a while—until their observing self develops and they can make wise choices—remains the best solution. Although moths are pretty, the world probably is not a lot worse off by losing a few moths to campfire flames or kerosene lamps. Losing a human being to self-destructive behaviors, however, is a tragedy.

Originally published in 1996.

24

Take Me Out to the Ballgame

recovery tool, perfectionism, positive outlook

Mike never felt he did things well enough. When he received a score of 98 on his math exam, he worried that he hadn't gotten 100. He was vice president of his class, but not president. He was chosen to play shortstop, but was not asked to be captain of his Little League team. You would think that receiving second prize on his science project would have been a source of pride, but to Mike it was a source of failure. Seeing how discouraged Mike was, his dad invited him to a ball game.

They took the train from their home in New Jersey into Manhattan and then caught the subway to the Bronx. When they exited at 161st Street, Mike couldn't believe the lights at Yankee Stadium. It seemed like the middle of the day. There were the monuments to the great Yankees of the past—Babe Ruth, Lou Gehrig, Joe DiMaggio, and others. It was great—but not great enough for Mike to forget his worries. Just before the game was going to begin, he couldn't stop thinking about being number two in his class, which wasn't good enough.

Soon the game began, and what an exciting game it was! In the third inning, the Red Sox pulled ahead, 2-0. The Yankees scored one run and then another. Boston scored again in the seventh inning, and the Yankees didn't have a chance to even it up until the end of the ninth. The designated hitter stepped up to bat and took a mighty swing. The ball went farther and farther, higher and higher—the hometown crowd was sure it would clear the right field fence. In the last second, however, with the wind blowing toward home plate, the ball fell slightly short and the right fielder snagged it for the final out.

On the way back to Manhattan, Mike and his father found seats on the downtown express, and they talked. "Mike, I want to ask you a question. What do you think of someone who fails more times then he succeeds?"

Mike said right away, "The guy's a loser." Dad then asked, "What if someone tries ten times and fails six or maybe even seven out of ten?"

Mike took off the Yankees cap his dad had bought him and scratched his head. "Dad, like I said, that's a terrible record. I feel bad when I get only nine out of ten on an exam. How could someone hold his head up when he's failing more than he's succeeding?"

Mike's dad put his arm around his shoulder and gave him a hug. "Son, think back to the game we just attended. They call someone who gets a hit four times out of ten a superstar. There are lots of times in life when you have to think of the context. Any baseball hitter with a record of .400 would certainly be voted Player of the Year. Let's think for a minute about how you are looking at yourself. You are looking at your failures, not your successes. You are a great guy, and you've got more going for you than the best hitter in the league. Why not look at what you are doing right and not at the times you strike out. After all, with your record, if you were a Yankee, you would be the most successful, most admired, best-paid member of the team!"

Comment

The old reference to whether you're looking at a glass half empty or half full seems worn out. Let's ask the question in another way. What President is famous for failing many times before he succeeded? The answer, of course, is Lincoln. If your perfectionist patients looked at their situations more objectively, they would be less discouraged, less self-critical, and more likely to give themselves the credit that is justly due. If Mike gave himself genuine praise, not flattery but praise, recognizing how well he had done, instead of turning the microscope on his perceived failures, he would be less vulnerable to developing problems like eating disorders. When nothing in life seems able to be done perfectly, it is tempting to find an area—such as weight loss—that can be done to exquisite perfection. No friend or teacher or coach can give as consistent praise as a scale showing you've gone down another pound.

Thomas Edison tried numerous ways to make an electric light bulb before he found the right way. Instead of criticizing himself for each "failure," he told himself that he was grateful he had found another idea he didn't have to think about so he could go on toward what he knew would be eventual success.

Hey, Mike, or Suzie, or Sam, or Joanie, remember that there are many situations in life where failing six times out of ten means you're the best in the league. Step up to bat, and take a swing at life.

Originally published in 1997.

25

Smoke Detector

bulimia, recovery tool, binge eating

One day Susan was standing in her kitchen cooking when she turned away to pet the dog. Since Max really looked as if he needed to go for a walk and do his business, she took him outside for a stroll. It was a beautiful day, with butterflies flitting around and hawks circling lazily in the sky. Fifteen or 20 minutes later, Susan headed home. When she entered the house, she heard the most awful buzzing sound. The oil in the frying pan had started smoking and filled the room with a pungent smell, as well as setting off the smoke detector.

Susan knew what to do, however. She took a broomstick and jabbed at the smoke detector. She poked it with all of her might until it finally stopped buzzing. She wiped her hands with satisfaction and said to herself, "Good riddance—its finally stopped," and was feeling she had taken care of that awful noise. When she turned around, she saw that the frying pan not only was sending off smoke but also had caught fire. Soon the room completely filled with dark smoke, and shortly after, the house burned down.

Comment

Let's not be too critical of Susan. I think of every bulimic urge as a

73

smoke detector sending off a signal that there is a fire going on somewhere that is generating smoke. Nobody in real life, of course, would attack the smoke detector for doing its job—giving off a signal that something was burning. If a patient with bulimic urges can step back and, instead of responding to the binge urge, see it as a kind of smoke detector, the bulimic urge can be a very helpful instrument. What do you do when the smoke detector is buzzing? You look around and see where the smoke is coming from. You find the source. You put out the fire, and when you do that, the buzzing stops—not because you have attacked the smoke detector, but because the source of the signal has been removed.

Bulimic urges come from a few sources, including hunger and habit, but most of the time, some emotional fire is smoldering. There is a problem that is sending off smoke, whether it is anxiety, anger, depression, being stuck, or being bored. A number of patients have found it helpful to become observers of their "smoke detector" (the bulimic urge) and investigate where the signal is coming from, rather than to go on with a binge.

Of course, it is not a completely good analogy, since destroying the smoke detector is not the same as a binge, but in many ways a binge does destroy information about the source of distress. If, instead, you can step back and say the binge urge is a signal that there is some intense emotion that needs to be located and dealt with in a healthy way, we can stop eradicating the binge urge by overeating, and instead use it as a direction finder for emotional distress.

Originally published in 1997.

26

Belly Up to the Bar

males, weight obsession, body image, thinness

Do you remember the wonderful intergalactic barroom in *Star Wars*, where Hans Solo and Chewbacca stride into the wildest bar scene on film? There are bizarre creatures from every part of the galaxy. Let's imagine how a man and woman might look for social companions at the Intergalactic Eating Disorders Bar, a place where we find a bizarre dress code.

In the first imaginary scene, Sam walks over to a section of the bar for men. He is convinced that his stomach is too big and the rest of his body too small, even though his weight is healthy. He feels lonely and hopes to find some social companions at the eating disorders intergalactic bar. Picture this: The guys sitting and standing at the bar are completely concealed except for a section exposing their mid-abdominal area, with slits for the eyes and mouth. Obviously, the first criterion for meeting a friend is a "six-pack" abdomen.

Sam walks along the bar, rejecting the first two patrons, because they have some obvious abdominal fat showing. The third person, however, Mordon, is a likely candidate for friendship; he has clearly defined rectus abdominus muscles, showing that he is a fit and lean potential friend.

Sam continues moving along, rejecting another bar visitor, who is thin and has no muscle development. Finally, on the 7th barstool, he finds an incredibly well-developed abdomen on Jnord. Sam invites these characters to join him at a table for some Martian-grown, low-fat snacks and pure water from the glaciers of Jupiter's largest moon. Sam is surprised when the six-packed Jnord pulls out a stun-gun and points it at him. At the same time, fit space-citizen Mordon robs him of his intergalactic passes for warp-speed transport and sends him into the next galaxy by way of a pulverizing worm hole. Then, they laugh at him.

Sue is also looking for friends and goes to the women's section of the Intergalactic Eating Disorders Bar. Women there are all covered except for the area from upper thigh to knee, which is good, because Sue obviously wants to relate only to people who have lean, muscular thighs that do not touch. Right away, on a barstool, she meets someone with fit quadriceps, Shanduras. A few stools down, she sees Alinotra from the Alpha Centuri neighborhood, who had lean, well-defined hamstrings, with clear separation between the thighs—another potential friend. Sue continues along the bar with some initial discouragement passing over several others until she finds another candidate for friendship, Juniece, who appears to not have a trace of fat on her thighs and has clear muscle definition. The three women proceed with Sue to a table to look at the nutrinos captured in the top of the hollow glass table. They order special vegetable juice from the Martian patches and, to celebrate, a cluster of bread baked from genetically engineered grain, grown on the north polar cap of the moon where water was recently found.

Sue does not notice when Shanduras slips a drug into her drink or that, while she is becoming drowsy, her new friend, Alinotra makes off with her purse and Juniece removes her gold jewelry from the rings of Saturn. Golly, by Jupiter, if you can't count on people who are fit and well defined—thin but muscular—to be your friends, who can you count on?

Comment

In a recent group for males with eating disorders, it was impressive how each person felt lonely and fat, even though their weights were below normal or in the normal range. The males in this group were all sensitive about their "big" abdomens. They believed the rest of their body to be too thin. They were very anxious about reaching out and making social friends. Because of their size and shape, they were sure they would be rejected by others. I suggested, in a somewhat disinhibited mood at the end of a workweek, that they should pick their friends on the basis of whether or not they had "six-pack" abs. They immediately rejected this idea. I asked them whether the people they were close to (usually just a few relatives or, sometimes, a patient friend) were valued because they had slim abdomens and mesomorphic muscle structure. They said, "Of course not." They liked the people they felt close to because these people were friendly, warm, accepting, and funny, shared their interests, etc. I asked them to imagine this wacko bar scene and challenged them to ask themselves if they would like to select friends on this basis of localized physical perfection. When they universally said "No," I suggested that others, likewise, would never select or reject them because of the size of their body or shape. On the other hand, they fear they will be teased or criticized for being the wrong size or shape.

Maybe I have watched Star Wars too much, but the intergalactic bar scene is wonderful and sticks in my mind. What an absurd idea it would be to go up to a bar and pick friends on the basis of exposed abdomens in men or thighs in women. Eating disorder patients would not use that absurd standard for valuing others and yet fear that others will use it toward them. Maybe a little imaging will help patients to see how unlikely it is that others will judge them based on their size, muscularity, or weight.

Originally published in 1997.

27

Big, Bad, Bertha and Innocent, Ineffective Ingrid

family dynamics, anorexia nervosa, personal power

Let's imagine that Angie sees herself in two very different roles. Angie is only 13. Sometimes she acts like big, bad "Bertha" and sometimes like innocent, ineffective "Ingrid." She does not have a multiple personality disorder, by the way, but recognizes that she acts out two very different roles as if she were both of these persons.

Toward her parents Angie is big bad Bertha—anything she says or does can have a tremendous negative impact on them. She is sure that when Dad is upset, she has caused it and needs to make it better. When Mom is down in the dumps, Bertha rubs her neck, smiles, makes her coffee, and even tucks her in, to cut down on Mom's excessive stress. Big bad Bertha knows that she has tremendous power—she can upset the adults around her. She can make them feel anxious and depressed or maybe even break up their marriage. This is a terrible power to have, and Bertha alone knows the harm she can cause if she does not act right or, heaven forbid, does something wrong. The problem is, she can never be sure she has done everything well enough, soon enough, or perfectly enough.

Angie plays out another role, however. This role is that of ineffective and innocent Ingrid. She seems to be completely ineffective. She is dependent on the care of others and is powerless to control others, much less herself. Sometimes, in fact, innocent, ineffective Ingrid would like to shrlnk into a speck of dust so she can't be seen or be hurt by others. There is just no way to change the world, to control others, or to protect herself. Why would anyone want to grow up? Maybe anorexia is the way to stop the clock, stop the treadmill, stop the confusion, shrink to nothing, and not have to worry about having the power of a wrecking ball (all damage). She believes she has the power to hurt others but has no power to help herself.

Comment

I treat a fair number of young children, beginning about age 12. They often have an overworked, distressing sense of their ability to do dreadful things. The children have "learned" that the quality of mom and dad's marriage, dad's stress-related temper and drinking, and mom's mood all depend on them. They are sure that if they do the wrong thing, or don't do the right thing, bad things will happen to the people around them—people they know, love, and depend on. It is a tremendous burden for a youngster to feel they are responsible for their parents' emotions and behavior

In marked contrast to this sense of negative power, the same person often feels utterly powerless about making good things happen—about nurturing themself, being assertive, and keeping boundaries between who is the parent and who is the kid.

I tell them: "You cannot have it both ways—you can't have so much electricity that you can electrocute someone and not enough electricity to light a little light bulb. You either have power or don't have power. You can't have all negative power and no positive power. The mathematics or physics just don't work out."

I challenge young people with this overworked sense of dread about the power and havoc they fear they have wreaked in others' lives, to look candidly at whether or not they truly have this power. I suggest they have perseverance if they have been able to drive their weight down to medically unhealthy anorexic levels and keep it that way. It is important for people to know that they may be very sensitive by nature, exquisitely tuned into the moods of others, but that does not mean that they are in charge. You simply cannot have all negative power and no positive power.

I encourage people to recognize what tremendous power they do have, but also the limitations. The power they really have is the power to understand themselves, to make sense of illness, to self-nurture, and to say "No. There is simply no way you can have the energy to blow up a city but not the energy to run a factory.

Let's dissolve, in our minds, the incompatible roles of big bad Bertha and innocent, ineffective Ingrid, and get back to being Angie, age 13. Let's help her develop an increasing sense of personal effectiveness—effectiveness to get on with a good life without an eating disorder, and having the power to cope with the challenges ahead in a truly adequate, nonperfectionistic, but satisfying and successful way.

Originally published in 1997.

28

Beds, Saws, and Suction

cosmetic surgery, thinness, males, weight obsession

A long time ago, during the era of Greek myths, there was a nasty character called Procrustes. This nasty character had the habit of doing rude things to people who came along. For instance, he was known to yank an innocent stranger from a road and stick this stranger into his bed. If the stranger were too short for the bed, he would stretch this person until he or she fit the bed, but if this stranger were too long, he would chop off the extra height.

Now, before you call him a lunatic, think about what we are doing to ourselves and our society. It is okay to be tall or short. No bed of Procrustes needed here. But heaven help you if you are a woman who is heavier than average or a man who is thinner than average. We are not much more modern than Procrustes!

Suzy is a 14-year-old girl with a bustline that would have been the envy of film stars of the 1950s. But that was a long time ago, so off Suzy goes to the plastic surgeon to have a breast reduction.

Sandra, on the other hand, has hips that her mother thinks are too large and thighs that her brothers tease her about. Presto, off to get liposuction. No more of this stretching or chopping of body parts as in the olden days. No, we put a catheter through the skin and suck out the unwanted fat, even if it is necessary for normal hormone functioning and perfectly safe. Are you a guy with a tummy ticking out? Then let's stick that tube under the skin to create an artificial six-pack of muscles.

How about Sam who is unhappy with his thinness and lack of upper body development? He can have silicone implants in his calves, the same done for his chest; and for his shoulders, he can have some of that extra fat tissue that others do not want. No, we would never do anything as unsophisticated and harmful as stretching people or chopping them short. We shrink or expand people today by methods only slightly less brutal than Procrustes. Weight and shape, not height, is the predominant concern for most people today.

Comment

When you "dust off" old stories, sometimes they are very contemporary. It is not clear why Procrustes had this inclination to standardize the height of everybody. It reminds me of an old cartoon, by Jules Feiffer, where four very different sized young men were entering a fraternity and by the last year, they all had been reduced or lengthened to the same height and had the same identical appearance.

Where do we get the idea that all women have to be thin? Now there is abundant evidence that weight is almost irrelevant unless you have diabetes, morbid obesity, or high blood pressure—provided you practice fitness. We have oversold thinness and undersold fitness and quality of life.

Originally published in 1997.

29

The Neon Sign

recovery tool, self expression, people pleasing

Once upon a time there was a little girl named Samantha who thought she was a neon sign.

When she felt lonely in her family, she was sure they would know she needed a hug or some warm words of encouragement. It was confusing and disappointing when others did not respond to her neon sign that said: "lonely—hugs needed—care for me."

When she had a thought that she considered shameful, like wishing her third grade teacher would die, she was mortified because she was again sure that the neon sign was telling people around her what she was thinking. When she developed a crush on Doug, even though she was careful not to show it in any behavior, she knew others could tell. Also, it was so hard to sit around the dinner table with thoughts in her mind about her developing figure, because she just knew others could tell what she was thinking about, and yet they were too polite to say anything.

One day in school, she left the girl's restroom without washing her hands and then just as she was walking into the classroom, she turned back, rushed into the girl's restroom and washed her hands thoroughly. She knew that when she returned to the class everyone would know she had not washed her hands, so better to do it now and then go back and try to avoid the laughter or snide comments she was sure they would make.

Samantha grew up this way and was usually unhappy or ashamed. To be a neon sign is a real burden—to feel deeply that you need the help of others and not receive it can only lead to disappointment and anger. To be sure that others can read your mind like a neon sign when you think something shameful, ugly, hateful, or even just sexy, is such an embarrassing problem.

When she eventually married Doug, their marriage was extremely difficult and lasted only a short time. One day as they were driving in the car, she said to him that it seemed kind of warm in the car, but he said that he thought it was comfortable. How he could not know she meant for him to roll down the window, she never understood. She felt strongly and deeply about it and was sure he must be ignoring her needs. Why couldn't he spend more time being close and affectionate?

After the divorce, Samantha took care of the kids on the weekdays and Doug had visitation on the weekends. Samantha never understood why the kids looked happy when they came back from Doug's house, even though she saw that he gave them hugs and kisses when he brought them home. Why didn't the children know she felt so strongly about her love for them? Anything she felt that strongly about had to be as obvious to the children as a blinking neon sign.

Eventually Samantha grew old and died. She left a note with her will telling how bitterly she suffered because others did not see her needs or notice how strongly she loved her family and friends. If she had been around, she would have been confused at the conversation of her friends and family after her death: "She was such a good woman, but we never knew what she thought or felt."

Comment

Many young people with anorexia seem to think they are a neon sign. This gets them into trouble two ways. First, they expect that others can see their needs and respond to them. After all, telling someone what you need is like begging, and you wouldn't want it anyway if you have to ask for it. Thinking of yourself as a neon sign (of course we are not being literal here) also means you have to hide the embarrassment of knowing others can read your mind when you have anything less than 100% nice, kind, pure thoughts. At times you do wonder how people can know what you are thinking and yet act so friendly and pleasant. Remember, we are not talking about people with schizophrenia—this is not about thought projection or first rank symptoms of schizophrenia. This is about sensitive personalities who do not learn that, no matter how strong their thoughts or feelings, others do not know anything about them unless they are shown in their behavior. I suggest to patients sometimes that the only thing another person can see or understand about your thinking is what a television camera on the wall would record—your behavior, verbal or non-verbal.

Unless you ask for what you need, it is only by luck that you will get what you need. No one can know if you have an embarrassing or hateful thought or something that you simply want to try out in your thinking. It is both comforting and challenging to really believe and practice that only what you say clearly by words or behavior can others understand.

Thoughts are private, for good or for bad. So, we should teach our patients to be clear and specific in communicating their needs and not to worry if some of their thoughts might best stay private. We are, after all, not neon signs.

Originally published in 1997.

30

Water

anorexia nervosa, nutritional rehabilitation

Jill was fortunate because her grandparents had given her money for a trip to Egypt to see the ancient ruins, pyramids, and the Sphinx. Jill liked the visit so much that she went on to obtain an archaeology degree. During her graduate work in Egypt, she struck out on an independent investigation and soon made an amazing discovery. She was following what others thought was a blind alley, a seemingly blocked tunnel leading away from the side of a pyramid. She noticed signs of a long-neglected doorway. After scraping away the sand, she discovered a tunnel leading to a chamber of a lost civilization that no one before had found.

The tunnel led not simply to the remains of an old royal family, but to a whole underground city, a civilization that had been unseen since its demise. What was amazing, however, was that the civilization could barely be recognized because all of its remains were dried and shrunken like a dry sponge.

Jill entered this city and saw the flattened remains of palm trees, the shrunken and dried remnants of plants and animals. There was an ancient housecat, flattened almost into a two-dimensional relief, with its paw out, batting at a ball of twine. What Jill was unprepared for was the chamber around the bend. Here was a whole family from the ancient world, barely recognizable because all that remained was its flattened, shrunken outline from many thousands of years ago.

What brought Jill international fame wasn't the discovery, but what she did next. Jill thought that this civilization had dried out and shrunken to almost a shadow of its former self because all the water (which constitutes 70% of life forms) had evaporated. She asked herself, What if I added water to this civilization? All the people that used to live here looked alike now—a white-gray color, with few distinguishing features. Jill secretly left the tunnel and the chambers and brought down a hose with water from a nearby oasis. As she sprinkled these life forms with water, they began to reemerge, and she did what no one else had ever done: She brought back to life an ancient civilization. The flattened housecat fluffed up, growled, and played with the ball of twine. A young girl who had been sitting at a potter's wheel developed form and color and soon was spinning the wheel again, finishing the clay pot that had sat frozen in time. She was now an attractive girl with dark black hair, cut straight across, and almost touching her shoulders. Her dark brown eyes sparkled again, and her deep caramel-colored skin reemerged. A boy who had been digging a row of beans filled out until his muscles grew back and a determined smile appeared on his face—and he went back to tilling his row. Jill kept applying the life-restoring water until a whole civilization returned from the flattened, dried-out images that she had discovered.

Comment

Treating anorexia nervosa patients is a lot like bringing dried sponges back to life. When they are very ill, most patients get a similar gaunt look, and most individuality is lost. The typical patient is bony, lacking in emotional expression, stereotyped in behaviors, and a shadow of her or his former self. When life-giving nutrition is taken in, each person goes on to reemerge as though a butterfly were coming out of a cocoon.

WATER

The seemingly identical, starved, emotionless, wooden-like clones go on to become Suzy, Sally, Jim, Andre, Aisha, or Yolanda.

Adequately nourishing anorexia patients is like putting water on dried-out sponges. As the essential missing ingredient is taken in, the similar-looking shadows of their former selves go on to develop individuality, color, life, and personality. It is like bringing an ancient civilization back to life. Sure, there is much other work to be done, but with re-nutrition, they emerge to become the persons they once were. The challenge then is to go down the path of wholeness, identity, and three-dimensional life.

Originally published in 1997.

31

Quality Not Quantity

family dynamics, quality of life, compulsivity

Ted and Mary were a busy, double-income professional family. They each had worked hard to earn their degrees, and now it was time to move up the ladder in their respective positions. They were a very modern couple, because they knew that with regard to time for family, it's quality—not quantity—that counts. They read all manner of recent studies and advice that showed that the intensity of the time, and quality of the time, with children is what counts. Let's see what happened when they followed this idea to its logical conclusion.

Ted and Mary planned to visit with their children for 1 hour every other Monday, Wednesday and Friday, and on every fourth Sunday afternoon between 2:OO and 4:OO. They always picked, in advance, something especially interesting for the children, whether it was reading a story, going for a walk in the park, or looking at a new video game together. After their quality interaction, the parents went out to their favorite restaurant and ate filet mignon, some french fries, and green beans that were still slightly crunchy. They ordered apple tart for dessert. The chef prepared each item perfectly. The waiter served their dinner, and each received 1 oz. of perfectly cooked, medium-rare steak, one french fry, one green bean, and a teaspoon of superb apple tart (remember, quality, not quantity).

After returning home and paying the babysitter, they slipped into bed for a time of romance. They timed themselves to be sure that they each gave and received two warm kisses, and their sexual encounter lasted a meaningful, intense, and high-quality two minutes.

One weekend their schedule called for the two of them to attend a great jazz concert. They knew the group would play mellow jazz with just the right touch and balance between bass, drums, and vocals. They had front-row seats. The audience erupted in applause when the group started to play. After ten minutes, plus a one-minute encore, the concert ended, and they were thrilled that band had played so incredibly well.

After the concert, Ted and Mary returned home for a one-minute meditation on the larger issues of life and then went to sleep with the satisfaction that they were not slaves to out-of-date ideas of quantity, but were sticking strictly with quality. Their divorce two years later was bitter, and surprisingly drawn out after they found out that each was having long, relaxed affairs with significant others. Their friends were not shocked. Their children never actually noticed that their parents were divorced.

Comment

Individuals need quantity as well as quality time alone to grow and develop. Couples need quantity as well as quality time to get to know each other and to foster the development of their relationship. Children need quantity as well as quality time with parents. Increasingly, dual-income professional couples give time, energy, and emotional investment to their jobs with leftovers for their relationships with each other and with their children. The idea that quality without any reference to quantity is sufficient is an illusion. Ask yourself, if you treated your job the way you treat your marriage or the relationship with your children, would your job prosper or decline? The monkey can't get its hand out of the jar unless it lets go of some of the bright shining pennies it is holding in its fist.

Originally published in 1997.

32

Ripples from Stones in Emotional Pools

all ED, quality of life, anxiety

Sam was determined to do things right and avoid any and all potential problems. He had the capacity to envisage the future and respond to it, even before it happened. For instance, he thought about his first day of high school and how the bully down the street might tease him. He felt the hot searing words coming at him, felt the nausea in his stomach, the color fading from his face, and the anger within. After an hour or so of experiencing this imagined event, he decided on a plan to avoid this by going in a side door at school.

Sam thought about his upcoming piano recital. He could envision himself starting well but then having his fingers become wet with perspiration and slip off the keyboard. Midway through, he would forget where he was and sit there in a panic, thinking about whether to start over or begin anywhere he could remember in the piece. He could feel the shame, the embarrassment, and the criticism from his family. Another few hours of practice each day and that would never happen.

He thought of asking Melissa to the first fall dance. He saw himself picking up the phone and asking her and then hearing her say, "Now, why would I want to go out with a nerd like you?" His reaction to this was anger, then sadness, and then despair. He went through the same scenario with each of the other girls he liked and felt himself responding to the words he was sure they would say. He decided then and there that he would not take the chance of asking any girl for a date.

Sam had difficulty falling asleep at night. He would think of what might happen if he got stuck in an elevator or on the plane ride he was supposed to take, imagining it ending in a fiery crash. He could even feel himself trying to crawl out of the flames over hot rivets but not able to find the exit. He left his first job interview and never went to see the personnel officer. He experienced, in advance, the rejection he was sure would come and decided to save himself the bother of all this emotional distress. Sam lived a long life. He experienced many, many terrible things during his imagined life, and a few of them actually happened.

Comment

Mark Twain apparently said he had experienced many terrible things in his life and some of those things actually happened. When we throw stones into a pool, there are ripples. When we throw emotional stones into emotional pools, there are ripples as well. Sometimes being too much in your head isn't so good. It is especially not good if you anticipate situations of defeat, disaster, embarrassment, rejection, humiliation, and loss, because the brain responds to those ideational situations as if they were real-life situations. Sam and others can go through all of the neurotransmitter responses of increased norepinephrine, dopamine release, elevated blood pressure, autonemic arousal, vasoconstriction in the periphery, and so on, from throwing emotional stones into emotional pools.

Sometimes it helps patients to ask if they can stop the ripples from spreading out after they have thrown a stone into a pool. It doesn't work when a kid sits by a lake throwing a stone into the water. You can't call the ripples back. They spread out to the other side of the lake. Emotional stones are just as likely to produce ripples that keep on spreading. The suffering from anticipated bad events keeps on spreading and produces changes for hours, days, and sometimes weeks later, as if the feared events had actually happened. If ideational work can be therapeutic in healing distressed ways of thinking, it can be damaging in other situations in which feared events are lived through in the mind as much as if they had taken place in real life. Preparation for probable events is different from emotional distress at imagining every possible future event. The ancients, as usual, had a saying for this situation: We pant because we walk on the shadows of mountains.

Originally published in 1998.

33

Saints Alive

anorexia nervosa, thinness

Once upon a time there was a 16-year-old girl named Maria, who lived near Avila, Spain, in the late 1500s. Her older sister had married at 17 and had three children. Maria's mother, Sofia, was worn down helping with grandchildren and still taking care of Maria's five younger siblings. Lent was coming, and Maria began to take seriously the diary of Teresa of Avila that her priest had been reading during the Lenten Masses. She fasted with even more severity this Lent to become holier, and followed her mother's example of going to Mass every day. On Fridays, she took in only water, and during the other days a single bowl of soup. She slept on straw.

When Easter came, Maria did not feast, however, but continued her practices of mortifying the flesh and saying novenas. Her priest noticed her among the many village young girls and commented on her spirituality. He observed her fasting and praying and denying herself. When next Easter came and Maria was even thinner than the year before, but with an intense radiance and a strong sense of holiness, her priest told the bishop, who invited her for a meeting. There he enlisted her support against the uprising by Protestants and asked her to pray for the souls of the wayward. She gave part of her food to the poor, lived Sundays only on the wafer at Mass, and spent hours kneeling until her knees were bloody.

Over the years, people began to ask Maria to intercede for them when they needed help with harvest or a family member was desperately ill. The bishop from time to time asked her for advice, and a report on her sanctity was sent to the Pope, who returned to her a special medal honoring holy women.

When Maria died peacefully at 27, she became a candidate for beatification. Her sister by then had 8 children and appeared many years older than her actual age. Her Mother had died at 44, leaving several young children. A diary of Maria's was found that described her desire to be holy by becoming as thin as possible and living on as little as possible, sharing all her food with the poor. In her diary she renounced any thoughts of sexuality or marriage and said she was glad that her monthly curse had disappeared.

Comment

When I was first asked to review the book *Holy Anorexia*, by Rudolph Bell, I thought the thesis that some of the fasting medieval saints had a form of anorexia nervosa was farfetched. I think now that they did in fact have a form of anorexia, which is not limited to any single cultural motif but exists when any self-induced starvation leads to severe underweight and a resistance to efforts to restore weight, as well as having reproductive hormone abnormality. Some of the early Christian martyrs and Stylites in the Egyptian desert may have represented males with eating disorders. To suggest they had an eating disorder is not a commentary on medieval religion. It simply suggests that there are other cultures in which the achievement of thinness for religious purposes can produce a sense of identity, purpose, and effectiveness. This was especially needed in late medieval and renaissance days for women, whose only "hopes" were to look forward to endless labor, many children, and treatment as second-class citizens, sometimes scorned as temptations to males. Maria achieved something very special that most women of her age could not achieve: she had a personal sense of holiness, a sense of control over her life, did not have to follow her mother's or sister's hard lives, and was taken seriously by the power structure of that day.

No one needs to make a judgment as to the worthwhileness of Maria's spiritual journey. In fact, we can resonate with her today when the process of adolescence, just as much as ever, calls for the development of a sense of identity, of purpose, of effectiveness. In our society, thinness is not as much a route to holiness as to being respected, not teased, and improving self-esteem. Rest in peace, Maria. You achieved something very important, but at a very high price.

Originally published in 1998.

34

Cooking up a Storm

anorexia nervosa, males, quality of life

Jim tried out for the cross-country team in his sophomore year of high school. He enjoyed cheeseburgers and TV. At 5'8" tall, he weighed 160 pounds. The coach who evaluated him told him he needed to lose 30 pounds, and Jim soon cut out sweets, counted fat grams so he had no more than 5 per day, eliminated breakfast, had a salad for lunch, and avoided most suppers by saying that he had eaten well in school. Soon Jim was down to 120, being very lean and fast on the cross-country team, but with a tendency to fainting occasionally if he stood up quickly.

Jim showed some interesting changes at home. He began cooking up a storm. He had not taken seriously his few cooking classes in junior high, and he had almost forgotten he knew how to cook. He started buying cookbooks and deciding what the family would eat, how much, and when. Soon after he got up in the morning he began thinking about food and how he could prepare special meals for his family and friends. An all-red dinner for Valentine's Day; green for St. Patrick's Day; different kinds of eggs for Easter; red, white, and blue for the Fourth of July. As he fell asleep, he began to dream about food. Jim lost another 10 pounds, bringing him to 110. His father gained 15, mother gained 10, and his sister gained 20. They ate better than they ever had before. No meal was too complicated for him to prepare. He bought all the cookbooks in the local bookshop and subscribed to several gourmet magazines.

Jim applied to the Culinary Institute of America and began to plan for a career as a chef. He had finally found his purpose in life: cooking up a storm, southern cooking, gourmet cooking, ethnic cooking—cooking, cooking, cooking. What a life Jim had—food, which he feared more than anything, dominated his life,

Comment

The limbic system, with its central connection to the hypothalamus, does not know that the patient with anorexia nervosa is not really in the midst of a typical historical famine. Through hundreds of thousands of years, the human race has been prepared for bouts of starvation with many systems that go into action when there is inadequate food intake. The senses are alerted, the eyes keenly seek out signs of berries or rabbits rustling in the leaves, the ears are alert to the breaking of a twig from a wild turkey, the keen sense of smell picks up the first ripe fruit in the spring. Sleep is reduced, and the body is alerted to get what it desperately needs—enough energy to live daily and to have some in reserve for special challenges.

Americans in general don't have any problem relating to the idea that someone who is dying of thirst in the desert will think of nothing but water, look for an oasis on the horizon, and be alert to the trickling of a little desert pool. They in general discount the idea that there is a price to pay for restricting food intake. The studies on experimental starvation by Keys, Brozek, Henschel, Michelson, and Taylor showed that ordinary men with no career involvement in food start collecting recipes, thinking of food, and either hoarding food or gobbling it when they lose weight averaging more than a 20% decrease. The limbic system serves as the mediator.

Originally published in 1998.

35

The Three Tailors

recovery tool, body image, thinness

Once upon a time there was a very proud lady in the kingdom of Antili-pidemia. She received a coveted invitation to the king's ball and decided to command the most flattering dress in the kingdom for the grand event. There were three exceedingly talented tailors in the kingdom, who knew of the king's ball and the proud lady's desire to have the most flattering dress. They met and wagered amongst themselves which one of them would be chosen to make the ball gown. She invited the three tailors to a meeting at her castle and demanded that the dress should make her look like the most elegant woman in the kingdom. She was shown fabrics from around the world and selected a silver silk cloth from China, with gold threads woven into the fabric, highlighted with the thistle flower insignia of the kingdom. Her measurements were taken by a discreet seamstress and given to each tailor. The three tailors worked in secret until the day when the proud lady would choose one of their creations.

On the day before the ball, the three tailors returned to her castle. Each tailor showed her his ball gown and explained why she should choose his work. The first tailor, named L-Mart, grandly spread out the floor-length gown with empire waist and scooped neckline, cut on the bias, adding that his dress, size 10, was made most economically and would cost only 100 gold florins. The second tailor, named Kacys, excitedly exclaimed that his floor-length gown with empire waist and scooped neckline, cut on the bias, was size 8 and, because of the great care with which the fabric was sewn, would cost 200 florins. The third tailor, named Treeman-Larcus, was confident that his grand chef d'oeuvre, a floor-length gown with empire waist and scooped neckline, cut on the bias, would be chosen. It was, after all, a size 2 and, without further explanation, added it would cost 1,000 gold florins.

The proud lady adjusted her looking glass, peered closely at each ball gown and, after deliberation, stated without hesitation that the Treeman-Larcus dress was clearly superior. At the ball, the proud lady confidently danced away the night, holding her head high, knowing that her ball gown was certainly the most flattering in the kingdom. In the meantime, the three tailors met at a local tavern to commiserate and to celebrate the results of their contest. L-Mart and Kacys knew what they had to do to win the next contest, while the third tailor decided that size 2 was probably too high a number for the proud lady's next gown.

Comment:

Too many women believe that the size of an article of clothing determines its worth. A dress in a store, patronized mostly by businesswomen may be marked size 6, will cost twice as much as a similarly fitting, identically cut dress from a budget store marked size 8. It is very strange indeed how a size 8 on First Avenue becomes a size 6 on Lexington Avenue and a size 4 on Madison Avenue. It might be dangerous to keep on walking to Fifth Avenue. You might get into negative numbers and disappear completely!

Originally published in 1998.

36

A Six-Pack Please

males, body image, teasing

Chuck had had enough teasing. Since childhood he had endured comments about his weight from his father, friends, and even random strangers, especially about his TTO (tummy ticking out). When he became a teen-ager and asked a girl to the high school junior prom, he was emotionally devastated when she said no because she would be embarrassed to be seen with a guy who had a "big gut." Chuck knew what he had to do. He started on a diet and an extreme exercise program. He would, like those sturdy hunks in the muscle magazines, finally have six-pack abdominal muscles with such definition that the separation between them could be seen clearly at a distance, muscle definition so obvious that any potential date for the senior prom would accept his invitation gladly. After all, everyone knew that groundwork for invitations to the prom began on the beach the summer before.

Chuck sweated and strained, increasing his time in the gym to 4, then 6, then 8 hours a day. He wanted to achieve that six-pack definition at any cost. He cut down his calories gradually to 1,000, then 800, then 400 a day. The fat melted away. He gradually began to see those elusive abdominals showing their striations. Of course, he also rapidly lost muscle mass in his legs, his chest, and his arms, but what the heck, that didn't matter, so long as he achieved abdominal definition. Finally, the month before the prom, he knew it was time to ask a date. He approached Sylvia, the raven-haired beauty, cheerleader, homecoming queen, and scholar of Latin and karate. He had rehearsed his speech and adopted a totally cool but sincere attitude, confident inside that his six-pack would speak for him.

Never before in her life had she seen a six-pack of diet cola shuffling along on its own like an android, gently nudging her ankle, and making speech-like sounds, including a question she had hoped to hear: "Will you come to the prom with me?" She knew that the originator of this clever and novel way of asking her to the prom had to be Chuck. She thought to herself, "That imaginative boy—he knows I love *Star Wars*. How cute of him to program an android to look like a six-pack of diet cola and program it to shuffle up to me and ask me to the prom. Of course I'll go with him." She walked over to Chuck and gave him a big hug and a kiss on the cheek, saying she would be glad to go the prom with him. He didn't know how she read his mind about wanting to take her to the prom, but he certainly wasn't going to turn down this acceptance from Sylvia. In the meantime, the six-pack of diet cola shuffled away. Most people thought the moisture on the six-pack was condensation, but a more perceptive person would know that even six-packs cry on occasion.

Comment

One of my colleagues, Dr. Kelly Brownell, chair of the Department of Psychology at Yale, once said that people with clearly defined six-packs for abdominals must be genetic mutants. He may have been kidding, but maybe not. As someone who couldn't demonstrate a six-pack if his life depended on it, I agree. Males have different but comparably disabling overvalued beliefs regarding their body size and shape than women— more shape than size concerns. Achieving a clearly defined six-pack has become an obsession with many young males—something to be achieved at any cost, even if it means self-starvation and wasting of the rest of the body, just so long as those abdominals match the magazine photos. Hugging a clearly defined six-pack of abdominals in a shape-obsessed young man is about as satisfying as hugging a cold six-pack of diet cola. We are more than our size and shape, certainly more than a stereotypical currently fashionable shape of a particular body part. Obsessing about muscles is valueless in achieving close human relationships. But I'm not sure you can convince a young man, who bears the emotional scars from teasing about abdominal obesity, that achieving a six-pack won't solve all his problems.

Originally published in 1998.

37

Worship Time

all ED, thinness, weight obsession, scales

Mary, Deb, and Sue all went to their respective religious services with their families, Mary to mass, Deb to temple, and Sue to morning service. In their families' respective religious services, they went through the motions, but in their hearts, they looked forward to their own meaningful religious experiences—the Grotto of Siam each Wednesday evening. On Wednesday evening at about bedtime, each of the three girls quietly sneaked out of her bedroom, leaving a pillow plumped up to look like a sleeping kid. They made their way to the Grotto, where they met other girls and a few guys coming from around town.

To enter the Grotto, each of them had to pass through a narrow entrance passage only 12 inches wide. If they were able to slide through sideways, they next had to pass the Electric Piggy Test. One by one, with hands folded in front of them, they stepped on a mildly electrified metal pad cut in the shape of a pig. Soon they felt a slight tingle as electricity measured their body fat. If the meter measured less than 10% body fat, they were allowed to proceed down the path to the Grotto. Once inside, they knelt in front of a large white object—the Scale of Life. It was shaped like the scale in a doctor's office but was about five times larger.

Before saying the weekly pledge, they heard a sermon from the Mistress of Thin: "You may have been reading in the popular press that there are 'good fats' in life. I'm here to tell you that this is heresy. There are no good fats, all are bad. Remember that a molecule on the lips is a lifetime on the hips. Fat molecules are slimy. They are ugly. They are dirty. They contaminate you. A pure life stays away from them. Be noble. Be clean. You do not want to disappoint the Scale of Life."

Then they said their weekly pledge: "I am not worthy to be in the presence of the Scale of Life and the Mistress of Thin. I have eaten more than 500 calories a day and I have let fat molecules pass my lips. I will exercise more. I will exercise at night, I will support my local laxative company. I will not rest until I have a Body Mass Index less than 16. I pledge myself to thinness, to happiness, and to the only meaningful judge of life—the Scale." Having said the pledge, they were led in their dismissal chant by the Mistress of Thin, an elegant woman 5 feet and 10 inches tall, 81 pounds, an object of true veneration. She said:

"Say after me: 'Oh, Wah.' That's good. Now feel your ribs, and say the second part of the chant: 'Tah, GOO.' Finally, say softly and with meaning the sacred third sound, 'Siam.'

"Now, ten times, fast, say the three sacred parts together, faster and faster, and then you will be prepared for this next week of living among the pigs, the bottom-feeders who eat cheeseburgers, the walking blobs of lard. Know that only you are good, only you are perfect, only you Grotto attenders are happy."

Comment

In Boy Scouts, we learned the chant above. Say all three phrases together, fast, and you will know what they mean. Our studies on the effect of eating disorders on religion show that, independent of the content of religion, eating disorders profoundly affect the religious and spiritual practices of patients. Fasting is increased. Roman Catholics with anorexia stay away from mass for fear of the number of calories in the wafer.

Bar mitzvahs are avoided because of the feasting. Fast days like Good Friday are extended far beyond their original purpose. I believe the desire for thinness is the most commonly shared and deeply held value among young girls, especially in this country. I don't think any religious or cultural belief is as deeply or as widely held. You have to take seriously and respect the power of something that can displace core existential beliefs in a higher power, supreme being, or other spiritual convictions. There is no particular religious causation of eating disorders, but there certainly is a spiritual aspect to this illness. An identity based on a dumb piece of metal that's given the power to judge us has to be less worthy than any of the widely practiced religious or spiritual traditions. The advice to patients to "get a life" would appropriately be understood to include "get some sort of a spiritual core beyond thinness."

Originally published in 1998.

38

Three Families

all ED, family dynamics

A new, remarkable technical development has allowed the public to overhear the language spoken by body organs. Through development of new microprocessors and Focal Amplification of Biological Systems (FABS), the following conversation was overheard in an obstetrician's office between three placentas. These three placentas came with their landladies for an appointment, each about 10 weeks after life had begun.

The first placenta introduced herself to her two fellow placentas. "My name is Darcy, Open Placenta Extraordinaire. I want to share with you my philosophy concerning my job. I take in everything that circulates through my system. I don't want to miss out on anything. My Precious Child needs to taste everything in life as early as possible. That's the best preparation for the outer world. I pick up and multiply anything that's swimming close to my big receptors and shoot it by the second messenger elevator shaft right to Precious Child's developing brain. I can't wait until my landlady goes to a coke and speed party this evening. There's a lot of heavy-duty mail coming my way, and I've got to see that Precious Child gets it all."

The second placenta was named Nina, Outraged Placenta Extraordinaire. "I hear you, Darcy, but that opinion scares me. I don't agree at all with your job description. I've already decided I'm going to make sure my Precious Child never gets exposed to anything that could hurt her development. My landlady is not very swift about everything. Sometimes she takes a second coffee in the morning, and once in a while, she hangs around holiday parties where the old office cronies smoke. I have instructed all of my membrane soldiers to guard the calcium channels so nothing questionable can come down the pike to Precious Child. I think my landlady shouldn't even have that extra tuna fish sandwich or the egg-white omelet she eats in the afternoon. That's too much protein, as far as I'm concerned. Someone has to protect Precious Child, and that's me."

Cora, Optimum Placenta Extraordinaire, was heard to respond to her two colleagues as follows. "You guys have me confused. I can't figure out whether Darcy or Nina is right. It's such a big responsibility, raising Precious Child. I just have to go about my business for the landlady the best I can and figure out which molecules coming by are keepers and which are throwbacks. I like to keep my membrane doors flexible. Sometimes I tell them they need to act like bouncers, and sometimes they need to put out the welcome mat. In fact, sometimes my membrane doorkeepers need to use a lasso and then a wheelchair, especially for those fast-moving folate frolickers that like to sneak by without a wave."

The next recorded conversation between these three organs occurred 30 weeks later, as the three placentas lay side by side in the lab adjoining the three delivery rooms. They looked somewhat like beached whales, or salmon that had spawned, but each was still able to converse, having completed her responsibility for raising Precious Child.

Darcy was crying and saying, "My Precious Child turned out to be such a disaster. She's big but all out of shape. Her eyes are close together. Her teeth are funny, she's shaking from not having me to give her her heroin, and two fingers are missing. I think I really blew it. But I tried to give her everything she wanted."

Nina was also pretty bummed out: "After all that hard work, you'd think I'd turn out more than a little two-pound runt with a hole at the end of her spinal cord. Just shows you what happens when you try hard. Shouldn't have bothered, Not worth it. See you guys."

Cora was also tired, but happy. "My Precious Child had an APGAR of 10 and settled down right away to feeding at the milk bar. She looked around with those bright eyes and was so cute when she wiggled her body and placed her perfectly formed hand in her mom's hand. You should have seen how happy the dad was, too."

Comment

When I studied the role of the placenta in protecting a fetal brain from abnormally high amino acid levels from congenital aminoacidemias, I quickly gained respect for the placenta. It was active and selective in its function—transmitting certain nutrients at the level of the mother's circulation, jacking up other levels like amino acids that the fetus needed more of, and screening out some substances. Individual cells in the body function in a similar way, as do the intestine and the blood-brain barrier.

Families are like these membranes or selective organ functions that govern much of the transport of material from outside the organ to inside the organ. The overly permissive family (D.O.P.E.) that lets all of society's craziness come into the family sets no boundaries ("Here, Precious Child, look at that Hollywood star snorting cocaine—that's so neat!") is more likely to produce a pseudo-adult child or very confused child who has no concept of boundaries or limits. Impulses are to be gratified, and emotional need, not thoughtful judgment, governs choices. This is a good breeding ground for bulimia nervosa.

The overly restrictive family (N.O.P.E.), in its worry to screen out everything harmful, also screens out good external elements and raises a hothouse Precious Child who only knows fear or the converse, rebellion. This child becomes permanently stunted in emotional and intellectual development and serves as a developmental matrix for anorexia nervosa, restricting subtype.

The balanced family (C.O.P.E.) makes judgments about what things are appropriate for growing members of the family. For example, it decides how much junk food is okay, how many hours of TV are reasonable, which songs have reasonable words and which are offensive, and it teaches Precious Child the difference between legal, moral fun and illegal, immoral activity. Precious Child learns to make judgments about the outer world without fearing it, but without over-idealizing trends and fashions, either.

May all families be selective and act like Cora. Is your family a D.O.P.E., a N.O.P.E., or a C.O.P.E.?

Originally published in 1998.

39

Top Gunner

weight obsession, bulimia, recovery tool

Juanita was the military's first candidate to be the new F-23 fighter pilot. Her fellow trainers kidded Juanita about being a Top Gunnette, but she put them in place pleasantly but firmly, saying "Hey guys, let's keep this strictly professional—performance, not gender, is what's going to save our necks over the combat zone."

Juanita wondered if her new fight suit was getting too tight. She had eaten too much last night with her pals—nobody had noticed when she slipped out to the ladies' room to get rid of it. Everyone was real cool. The kiss of death for this kind of training would be to say you were anxious. Top Guns and Gunnettes are rational thinking machines and, when necessary, killing machines. She'd eventually even the score somewhere for her father's death in Vietnam and for that guy who took advantage of her after slipping her a "roofie." No time for that. It's training time.

Juanita sat at the flight simulator and noticed something strange. Only one dial was visible. It was labeled F.A.T. (flight avionics tachistoscope). On one end of the red line across the center of the dial was the word Low and on the other end High. Oh well, she thought, I suppose it's like skiing— start with limited equipment, learn it right, then add the extras. Pressing down on the red start button, she gunned the engine. It made a roar just like the F-23 she'd heard at the demo last month. Now, with her right hand on the joystick, she guided the awesome machine up toward cruise altitude. Funny thing, though, suddenly the plane tilted to the right and began a long death spiral that ended up in a big splat on the computer screen. All the way down, the red dial kept moving closer toward High, until it was in the extreme-danger zone at the time of the crash. Luckily, this was just a simulator.

OK, let's try again. Can't expect perfection first time around. This time, she restarted the engine and nosed it a bit more gently up in altitude. I can't believe this, she said to herself, as she saw the red dial climbing for a second time toward the High reading and then into the extreme-danger zone. Only this time, the sound of the engines stopped. She had stalled out on the way up, and now the fighter was spiraling down to the left. Splat! There goes another 90 million bucks. Where were those other dials—the flap adjusters, the afterburner controls, the horizon bar, the altitude indicator, even the speed?

"Could I make a suggestion?" asked the trainer. I know you're very competent, but even Top Guns and Top Gunnettes need all their dials uncovered. So, instead of trying to do your first flight with only that F.A.T. dial, let's take the black sticky paper off those other dials and uncover the altimeter, the horizon bar, your speed indicator, and the other dials on the information panel you'll need for a successful flight. Let's get going, Juanita—see you in the skies. I know you can do it."

Comment

Feelings (really, thoughts) of fatness are in many ways a common denominator for a variety of powerful forces—especially hunger and dysphoric moods. The problem comes when the only dial that registers on the personal emotional distress instrument panel is, "I feel fat—a little, a bit more, even more, and extreme." I've found it useful to suggest to patients that they consider the thought that they are fat to be so strong because that's the only dial they are reading. The other personal dials need to be uncovered and the readings noticed. For example, if a person has the thought "I feel fat" and then has the urge to skip a meal, or to binge, followed by a purge, I ask them to slow down the process, take time to answer the question, "If you couldn't use the words 'I feel fat,' what other words would you use? Hungry, anxious, angry, sad, stuck, bored, lonely?" Try taking the fat word out of your vocabulary, look at the other dials, and see what's really reading in the danger zone. What you do about being anxious is different from what you do about being angry or sad. It helps to fly reading all your dials. Looking only at the dial for "I feel fat—a little or a lot" is like trying to fly a jet on one nonspecific dial. The technical term is alexithymia: not being able to read feelings.

Whether it's a predisposing condition or a consequence of having all of life focused on the perception of body fatness isn't a settled issue. What we do know is that accurately identifying the emotions that are really present lets you run your plane, your life, your jobs, to the best of your ability. Otherwise, it's crash landing time for Top Guns, Top Gunnettes, and everybody else. Let's get all those personal dials uncovered; start reading all of the flight panel instrument controls, and make the best moves to leading life safely and effectively. With all your instrument readings in front of you, you can take off safely, fly high, far, and fast and come back safely.

Originally published in 1999.

40

Georgette in the City of Light

perfectionism, compulsivity, quality of life

Georgette's dream had come true: She was in Paris, the city of lights and love, home of her ancestors. The plane arrived on time. She followed the rules for adapting to European time—get some sleep on the plane, walk out in the sunshine right after you arrive, eat some high-protein foods for breakfast and lunch, and go to bed on local time. The tour was scheduled to start the day after arrival with a bus trip to drive the group to a *bateau mouche* tour on the Seine for the beginning of a leisurely trip down the romantic river as it wended its way through Paris, flowing around the *Île de France*, with the beautiful Notre Dame Cathedral rising majestically from the eastern point of the island—you know, the cathedral made famous by the hunchback story. She almost couldn't stand the waiting. She was up at eight o'clock the day after arrival in order to catch the nine o'clock bus beginning the tour.

As she was dressing, she noticed that her shoes were not in order. It would take only a minute to have all the toes lined up. Blast it! Those dresses weren't arranged in order of descending lengths. That would take only another minute. Things didn't quite feel right yet. She couldn't leave her makeup kit in disorder. The lipsticks had to go on one side, the compact on the other. OK, so I get the ten o'clock bus and a later Seine tour. That was better than leaving the room with the feeling that things weren't symmetrical and organized. Finally she was ready to leave the room.

The trays from room service delivered the night before were laid in helter-skelter disarray outside the other rooms on the corridor to the elevator. *This is dumb,* she thought, but she knew she couldn't go to the elevator without pushing each tray back against the wall so that they were all even. You wouldn't believe the way the French left cigarette butts on the floor of the elevator. It wouldn't be a big problem to ride the elevator up again while she picked up the butts. Besides, there was an eleven o'clock bus. She walked confidently out of the elevator to her long-awaited tour. *Merde.* The flowers in that beautiful vase in the lobby needed just a little rearranging. It would never do in this classy place to have the flowers sticking out at all those different angles with the length of the flower stems showing no orderly progression. While the desk clerk looked away to take telephone calls, she poked her head up from behind the large lobby vase and rearranged the flowers one at a time until they went from shorter to longer, top to bottom, and all the color patterns were repeated in the same sequence on each side of the vase.

Too late for the tour. After all, who wants an organized tour? Paris is the city for enjoying things spontaneously as they come up. Might as well try out the restaurant in the lobby for lunch. Those forks aren't lined up. It would only take a few minutes to gently nudge the forks on the empty tables so they were lined up right, and the people coming to sit down wouldn't have to interrupt their *soupe á l'oignon* to do it themselves. By the time she had slowly and delicately consumed her *créme brulée,* it was getting a bit late, so she decided to stroll on her own. If only people hadn't thrown their umbrellas so randomly in the containers near the restaurant doors. Of course, she would not embarrass the bellhop who was casually smoking in between kisses with the stunning blonde just outside the door. She would rearrange the umbrellas herself. Finally, the only thing between her and savoring the city of love's visual delights was making sure the hotel business cards were gently tapped down in their holder near the door so people arriving wouldn't be upset by the lack of symmetry. It felt so much better compared to leaving them sticking up at different heights.

Napoleon did some things right—he and his architects commanded that the avenues be wide and radiate spoke-like from central monuments. He directed that the major buildings conform to classical French architecture with equally angled chateau-style roofs. It was wonderful to finally be out in the late afternoon sun.

Should she go left or right? After all, she was on her own, and it didn't really matter. If she went right, she would walk toward the *Place de la Concorde*. If she went left, she would reach the Louvre in a few blocks. *Place de la Concorde* was certainly an historic place. That beautiful obelisk. Just think, more obelisks in Paris than in Egypt. But then again, the Louvre was probably the most distinguished museum in the world. That new entrance by I. M. Pei was so typically Parisian—just like the Eiffel tower, hated at first, but gradually much beloved and eventually so much a part of the landscape that no one could imagine the city without it. But who wants to be inside a museum on a beautiful evening. Then again, the museum has an outdoor sculpture court near the *École des Beaux Arts* at the western end of the Louvre. This was the perfect compromise; worth taking a bit of time to think things through. After all, this trip was what she had been saving for and preparing for.

After several hours of intense decision-making about whether to go left or right, the clock in the nearby church bell tower struck midnight. No one can tell me that there is anything more beautiful than a walk around the hotel block at midnight. Life was good. Everything was in order. There's always tomorrow, or maybe the day after, to do that tour. If only that tour booklet didn't have the red and blue squares on the cover at different heights. Who cares. After all, I'm in Paris.

Comment

Obsessive-compulsive personality features are common in eating disorders, perhaps essential to developing restricting anorexia nervosa. Life has to be hard when every neuron is screaming at you: Keep it symmetrical, make sure everything is in order, square those corners, don't worry if others think you're overdoing it.

Although the debate is far from being settled, it looks like some degree of obsessive-compulsive trait, if not a full Cluster C personality disorder, is essential to being a competent anorexic. Unfortunately, the world is not always a neat place. Wisdom often consists in learning what to ignore. If you have significant obsessive-compulsive traits or disorder, life becomes a struggle between the relentlessness of entropy versus your disorder's needs for organizing. So many things in life are missed if everything has to be symmetrical or in absolute order. What about this personality feature is "hard wiring" and what is a consequence of the illness remains unanswered. But what is clear is that many patients with eating disorders, especially anorexia nervosa, will need help not only in treatment of nutritional neglect but also in freeing themselves from a desire to have things impossibly ordered or symmetrical. Randomness, chaos, and moderate order, rather than absolute order, are part of a normal life. Let's leave perfection to neurosurgeons and pilots of wide-body planes. For the rest of life, anything worth doing is worth doing "badly." Perfectionism is generally overrated, while adequacy and reasonable standards are healthy goals.

Originally published in 1999.

41

Tiny Tim or Big Ben?

males, body image, steroids

Once upon a time, there was a boy named Ben, a classical ectomorph.

Ben was sick of being teased about his beanpole physique. He was sick and tired of having sand kicked in his face at the beach by some big bully with biceps the size of hams and pecs like they were carved out of granite. He read every fitness magazine he could find and secretly joined a grungy gym, where the big boys worked out. He did push-ups every morning and lifted bags of cement on his part-time job in construction. Soon he found a beaten up tank top and shorts that made him look like a gym rat. Without looking interested, he listened in on the guys' conversations about how to bulk up. He went on a high protein diet, like the most pumped up lifters, and by joining two different gyms, no one would see how much he exercised.

Gradually, his body became transformed. Eventually, Ben could pass as a model for Michaelangelo's David, but that was nothing but a pause on the way to his goal of being the biggest, most cut, ripped, shredded hunk. It was clear that lifting iron and high protein meals wouldn't cut it. It was time for chemistry. The DHEA helped a bit, and so did the creatine, but he needed more juice. When he looked chiseled enough not to be totally ashamed of his body, he introduced himself to the guys with the biggest pecs at the gym. There he traded his construction paycheck for a real stack: diabinol, winstrol, and oral testosterone. When his chest passed 50 inches and his waist was 32 inches, he still was sure he was a puny little thug. Soon he doubled the stack of steroids, and really began to grow. Soon, he wasn't able to walk through doors without turning sideways. His neck was 22 inches, his biceps 24 inches, and the legs were too massive for any pair of jeans.

Yet, every day when he looked in the mirror, he saw puny piano legs, a sunken chest, and scrawny chicken neck. What the heck was he going to do? He doubled the weights and began to enter tractor pulls in which he was on one end of the rope, and a tractor on the other. The tough guys at the gym no longer gave him a hard time. He started lifting compact cars and then moved on to hoisting vans and limos.

"I'm just a tiny Tim, and I'll always be that way," he said as he weighed himself and found he was just shy of 400 pounds. A guy he threatened with just a little pressure around the neck stole some growth hormone from the hospital lab to pass on to him, and that helped a little. The only thing that didn't get bigger was his nuts, which now fitted into small skivvies. He checked his profile in each mirror he walked by, and he noted his reflection in shop windows. "Blast it, why am I so small? I've got to bulk up. I don't know if I can go on being so tiny. Life just isn't worth living like this. I know they'll tell me I look good, but they really mean I'm a shrimp." Other guys at the gym started saying "Here comes Big Ben." He started wearing a loose sweatshirt to hide his enlarged nipples. Finally, he couldn't stand it any more and went on a protein-only diet, quadrupling his anabolic steroid stack, and increasing his time in the gym to 10 hours a day.

During a weightlifting contest for strongest man in all the land, he suddenly collapsed while trying to set a new world record. The autopsy showed only 2% body fat, clogged coronary arteries, a blown-out middle cerebral artery, a cirrhotic liver, shrunken testes, and enlarged nipples. But his abs and pecs had amazing definition.

Comment

Eating disorders are characterized by body image distortion, most commonly the perception (not a delusion, but a perceptual distortion) that the person is fat despite being thin or actually starved in appearance. When a 65-pound woman of average height pulls out an intravenous drip because she sees there is some glucose in the solution, saying, "You're not going to make me fat," that's perceptual distortion.

There is no reason that perceptual distortion has to go in one direction only. I have hypothesized that males especially might feel that they are too small, despite being bulked up. Recent reports of "reverse anorexia" or "muscle dysmorphia" have confirmed that phenomenon. It exists primarily in men—and in many ways is the reverse of anorexia nervosa—but in this case, nothing is big enough. Males who never think they are big enough are more liable to misuse anabolic steroids and other chemicals to bulk up. Reverse anorexia can be just as disabling as anorexia nervosa, because nothing is big enough.

Originally published in 1999.

42

Neither a Borrower nor a Lender Be

bulimia, impulsivity

"No, Francine, you simply cannot borrow any more. Your account is way overdrawn. Even our bank has limits. Please reconsider your request."

"Yes, Mr. Argent, I understand. But this is really important. Let me explain why I need to borrow some more. You see, everything is so quiet now. I can't stand it. I need to borrow some trouble. I'm desperate and you are my last hope. I promise, I will pay you back."

"I don't know why I put up with this. Well, one last time. How many trouble credits do you need?"

"Okay, since this is my last loan, let me put it on the line. I need about a thousand units of trouble credit. Believe me, I won't ask again."

"How in the world can you spend a thousand trouble credits?"

"I have a very organized plan. I'm sure you and the Trouble Credit Board will support me. They won't be spent in one big lump. Don't worry. Let me explain. First, there's the meeting with my Aunt Gladys. She's been sending me these sweet notes. If I bring up her icky divorce at the family reunion, she'll explode, and those sappy notes will stop. Then, when my cousin Vanessa sees me, I know she'll say I look good, but I'll tell her she's just being nice, and I know in her heart she thinks I'm ugly."

"You do seem to have a plan, Francine. Go on."

"I've been trying to go farther and farther on a tank of gas. If I keep stretching out my driving past the empty point on the dial, I'll find out just how much gas I have. The highway isn't that busy at midnight, and sometimes the state police drive by. Or else, one of those nice guys in a pickup truck may help me."

"Well, Francine, that accounts for about 500 trouble credits. You still have to explain your plan for the next 500 you want to borrow."

"Let me try, Mr. Argent. There's a term paper due for my history class. I think I'll write it on why the Holocaust never existed, and that the Holocaust is a plot by Zionist extremists to create sympathy. I know it's not true, but it'll sure stir people up. Then I have a date with Brad on Saturday night. I won't go out with him if he's been mainlining, but if its only pot and meth, we'll be fine. He's wanted to have unprotected sex. He says it feels so much better, and if I really care for him, I'll go along. He's probably right. I had thought of standing up in a movie theater showing one of these films about bugs and shouting that I smell smoke. It would be fun to see the audience act like a bunch of ants being attacked by an anteater. But, instead, I think I'll run up a bunch of bills in Las Vegas and on Rodeo Drive and then declare bankruptcy. I'm almost ready to do it anyway. So that accounts for 800 trouble units.

"You've got to give me some flexibility to use the rest creatively as situations come along—after all, there's only 20% unaccounted for. Think of the possibilities of literally skating on thin ice by trying some forbidden late spring skating on the pond after the No Trespassing sign is put out. Then, there's the fantastically funny idea of letting the neighbor's Rotweiller out when the kids walk home from school. When things get really dull, I can do the false alarm with the fire station. Please, Mr. Argent, give me a chance."

"Francine, you've convinced me. We will advance you one thousand trouble credits. But we will be watching to see that you use them as you have planned. And then there's the payback. The usual terms will apply."

"Of course, Mr. Argent. Thank you so much. You can count on me. You don't know how much this means to me." And then, *sotto voce,* "Just try to get me to pay it back. See you, chum."

Comment

There is an old folk saying, "Don't borrow trouble." You'd think that borrowing would be limited to things that people really need—like money for health care, education, a special trip, or a home purchase. But there are people who desperately need to borrow trouble. If things are calm, if there is no risk, no danger, no stirred-up family relationships, just plain old safe sex, why bother. Let's get the wherewithal to make things rock—to destabilize stable situations that bore the heck out of some people. For them, life without trouble—unreasonable risk and tension—is a life not worth living.

There is a payback for borrowing trouble—it's called *more trouble.* The classic histrionic personality exists calmly only when surrounded by a swirling hurricane of colliding caregivers, while the person surveys the situation from the quiet eye of the storm. Some bulimia nervosa patients have a problem only with binge behavior, and once that's better they're on their way. But for many bulimia nervosa patients, the eating disorder is only one aspect of a multi-impulsive personality disorder that is excitement seeking and is strangely distressed in the midst of calm, order, and harmony. Unfortunately, there are too many banks willing to lend trouble credits.

Originally published in 1999.

43

Trapeze

all ED, recovery tool, letting go

Zolo was an aspiring circus artist, perfecting her trapeze act. Finally, the big night had come to star in front of an audience. Crowds filled the tent. The smell of popcorn and sawdust permeated the air. Tigers were pacing in their cage knowing they would soon hear the crack of a whip. The sideshow had all the usual oddities.

When her time came, Zolo mounted the tall, narrow rope ladder up to her platform. Lights dimmed. The band played a rousing chorus and then suddenly stopped. The spotlight caught Zolo's sequined outfit as it sparkled in the spotlight. Zolo unhooked her trapeze swing, leaned back, looked around at the crowd, and then launched into space. From the opposite side, an empty trapeze swing was gently pushed at the same time. At the critical meeting point, in the center of the arena, she would let go of her swing, fly through space for several feet, grab the oncoming swing, and ride safely to the opposite platform, landing safely, while basking in applause.

She felt the air rushing by her, her adrenaline surging, her heart pounding. At the critical moment, her hands seemed to cling to her swing as if glued there. Soon, she felt herself carried by momentum back to her starting platform. The crowd thought this was a great teaser. They gasped, and then settled down for the real transfer—the second one. They knew now that the first one was just to get them warmed up. This was circus artistry at its best—trick the crowd and leave them wanting more than ever to see her daring performance. She took another deep breath. The band played the chorus, then stopped. Drum roll...she left the platform to hurtle through the air. Again, at the meeting point, her fingers froze and she returned to her original platform. This time, Zola turned silently, slipped awkwardly down the rope ladder, hurried into the night and disappeared forever.

Comment

The treatment of eating disorders involves many components—the nutritional and medical aspects are challenging, but generally straightforward. The core issue comes when it is time for the patient to let go of the eating disordered identity and grab hold of a new life of health, daring to transfer from the illness trapeze onto a new swing to wholeness. This process is scary—much like letting go of the first trapeze and grabbing on to the other—requiring first letting go and hurtling through space. Even though the mind says it's okay, the transfer—to truly let go of sickness and grab on to a new way of life—is frightening. It's a risk in many ways—an existential one, especially. The gap seems large, the fall probable, and the security of the first platform increasingly comfortable. There is only one healthy alternative, however, to let go of illness and take hold of a new life. The other option is to slip away into the darkness of continued illness.

Originally published in 1999.

44

Sticks and Stones

males, teasing, body image

Luke and Matt were fraternal twins. You would guess they were from different planets by the way they looked and acted. Luke was fair, sensitive, kind to a fault, with a medium paunch. Matt was broad-shouldered, athletic, usually putting himself first in everything, and had a vicious sense of humor.

On the same day, very different things happened to Luke and Matt. When Luke was in the fifth grade, he was surrounded by a bunch of sixth-grade bullies dressed in baggy jeans with crotches that reached the knees and shirts with four-letter words printed on them. "You're a fat pig, Luke. You're nothing but a ton of lard. You look like a beached whale. Are you sure you don't need a wheelbarrow for that gut?" While this was happening, Matt was climbing the school water tower to put a team pennant at the top before the homecoming game. He decided to show off on the way down, and by using his extraordinary trapezius and arm muscles, tried to lower himself down the water tower using only his hands, with his legs spread out in a V straddling the ladder. About 20 feet from the ground, he encountered a patch of moisture and couldn't keep his grip. He tumbled down, breaking his shoulder, fracturing his left femur, and crushing one ankle.

Luke went home and started telling Dad about the teasing. His dad couldn't understand what it was all about, "Sticks and stones will break your bones, but names will never hurt you. Why don't you grow up, kid, and do something about that belly? You're too young for a belly. You're not even drinking yet. No kid of mine is going to be a fat wimp."

About that time, Dad got a call from the hospital saying that Matt was going in to emergency surgery. He rushed to the hospital and was able to talk with Matt for a while. The doctors assured him that even though Matt had several breaks, modern techniques would allow for good healing. "That's my boy, Matt. I don't know of any kid worth his salt who doesn't get a few breaks. Maybe it was a little dumb climbing that tower but I'm proud of you, son, for being an all-around jock. Those breaks must hurt a heck of a lot. I'm with you all the way. I'll make sure the doctors give you plenty of pain medicine. We'll see you through this."

When Luke was 15, he was teased because he would never be a "skin" when he played pickup basketball, but would only take part if he was sure he could be a "shirt." When he was 18, Julie turned him down for the prom and said she just couldn't imagine going with somebody so fat. Luke worked hard and hired a trainer. He enlisted in the Marine Corps, and his drill sergeant told him he probably wouldn't make it. He started cutting down on meals and increased his exercise until he was able to do 200 push-ups and 1,000 sit-ups. There was no trace of a belly, but Luke was sure he still had one. When he dieted from 180 pounds to 120, he was given a medical discharge from the Marines for having anorexia nervosa.

When his weight reached 105, his father was concerned enough to tell him to cut it out and eat normally. "Of course, don't become a pig like you were before, but put some meat on those bones. You look like the wimp I said you were going to be." In therapy, he found an understanding psychologist who was able to get him to change his thinking and behavior. It required several years, however, before he was able to let go of the image of himself as a fat kid, and especially those taunting words. If you think the words engraved on a stone tablet are firmly etched, you need to realize how deeply written in Luke's mind were words like "fat pig."

Matt's orthopedic injuries healed perfectly. It took some expert surgery to get his ankle back in shape. The femur required a pin, but the only residual problem was setting off metal detectors at the airport. His shoulder healed well and the separation was reunited without surgery. Matt went on to become a semipro football player. He broke several more bones and developed a permanent hobble after five years in the All-Canada League. He was incredibly grateful that his father had been with him that day he broke those bones. He never could understand what a sissy Luke became and still teased him at holiday get-togethers about what a fat little kid he used to be.

Comment

The phrase, "Sticks and stones will break your bones, but names will never hurt you," is completely wrong. Most bone breaks will heal well. With modern surgery and physical rehabilitation, it's amazing what specialists can do. In contrast, belittling words addressed to a growing guy who happens to have some extra weight—especially abdominal or breast weight during those vulnerable years (when "the concrete is still wet")—can do damage forever. Especially in a sensitive kid, teasing will go on to influence him in a way that most broken bones will never do. Bones heal, but cruel words rarely do. Therapy helps, sometimes eradicates them, but there is no splint for a broken spirit and no pin for a fractured self-esteem.

Originally published in 1999.

45

Jack and Jill Went Down the River

bulimia, sexual abuse, brain chemistry

Jack and Jill, one lazy summer day, went down to the upper Niagara River to race canoes against each other. In the new gender-neutral canoe teams at the local high school, the best rowers would be chosen for the team. It was a perfect summer day—fluffy white clouds moved like cotton candy, and with a little imagination you could find animals, faces, and islands floating in the sky. The river was not too cool either, since by August the summer sun had warmed up the water.

They launched happily into the river and they were paddling merrily along. Of course, having lived there all of their lives, they knew that they could only go so far before the current got too swift and the falls roared dangerously. Neither of them realized how strong they had gotten through their strength training over the past year. Jill's triceps were incredibly well-developed and her pectorals and trapezius handled the oars evenly as she switched the paddle from side to side. Jack was no slouch, either, and sometimes raced ahead of Jill and sometimes fell behind.

Soon they noticed that the current was beginning to pick up a bit and they saw the first signs on the side, which cautioned them about the falls in the distance ahead. "Well, we know this area well enough and we will turn around in good time; those signs are for tourists." They resumed their race, thinking about who would be the team captain. The sound in the distance became stronger and in fact felt more like a rumble than a sound. "Hey, Jill, let's turn back, let's call it a draw."

"Not on your life Jack. I know how to handle myself; you can chicken out if you want."

The water now began to be choppy. The current had a distinct pull to it. The sounds of the falls became louder. Suddenly Jack knew what he had to do. He paddled with all his might, diagonally making slow progress towards the shore but all the time being pulled further downstream. Finally, when the water was becoming a rushing current, he saw an overhanging branch, stood up, grabbed the branch, and moved himself hand over hand until he was on the shore and his empty canoe surged on ahead without him.

Jill thought that this was the time to show who was stronger. "Another 100 yards and I will do the same as Jack. He will be sorry he quit so soon." Jill tried to move her canoe to the side. It would not respond, however. The feeling was much like what you get when your pick-up truck on the farm is caught in a deep rut and you cannot get it back out. She tried paddling left and then right, but nothing helped. "I can't believe it," she said aloud to no one. Believe it or not, it happened. The canoe was swept straight down and over the falls. No amount of effort could change the ending. Luckily she landed in a pool of deep water and surfaced before the mighty stream carried her further down into the whirlpool. Eventually she made it into a quiet, calmer, shallower part of river where she could turn over on her back and slowly make her way to shore, with just enough energy to collapse on the bank.

Comment

Eating disorders are in many ways similar to what happens when a canoe paddler gets into a river headed for a falls or rapids. You get in voluntarily. You stroke along, perhaps getting a sense of excitement as you go further and further downstream, but if you stay in that river long enough, your journey is no longer a voluntary process. Eating disorders usually begin with self-induced starvation (i.e., diet) and a desire to lose a specified amount of weight. The process, however, has its own built-in momentum, not well understood, and perhaps fueled by serotoninergic mechanisms. At a certain point, self-directed efforts to get out of the river don't work any more. That is why there is special urgency in preventing a "canoeist" from entering this particular "river" of dieting. The transition of dieting into an involuntary disorder explains the importance of urging them to go to shore or going after them to bring them to shore before the current carries them further down and down. After a certain point, there is no longer the possibility of meaningful self-rescue.

Originally published in 2000.

46

Organ Language II

bulimia, sexual abuse, brain chemistry

This story was made possible by the scientific discovery of the modern computer's ability to directly modulate the neural activity of brain centers into a simulated voice using a 2-GIG-RAM, 80-TB hard disk memory to finally hear what brain nuclei say to each other. The Nobel Prize for this accomplishment wasn't long in coming for the discoverers of modulated brain center organ language. Possibilities of achieving this advance had been hinted at in psychodynamic papers a hundred years ago, in the 1930s, and also hypothesized by the early single-cell recordings during the 1960s. What an incredible understanding has come in the last century with this ability to intercept connections between brain centers. The following is an edited transcript of the first recorded conversation, between the amygdala, the hippocampus, and the frontal lobe in a patient, Evelyn.

Myg (Amygdala): "If you can't stand the heat, get out of the kitchen. When you give me those signals, you know what I have to do. The codons can't be changed."

Myg had been trying to answer the saltatory junction (SJ) mail from Frolob, the coordinator of the frontal lobe centers. Frolob kept complaining that she was getting burned by the cortisol and the epinephrine that LC (the locus ceruleus) commanded the adrenal to put out. That's not even mentioning the norepinephrine from the emergency peripheral nerves.

Frolob: "You won't believe how fried it feels up here in the frontal lobe—like an egg on hot concrete—when that cortisol doubles and sometimes triples. And that norepi tightens all those vessels so I barely get my glucose."

Myg: "You'd better check with Hip (hippocampus). He's giving the directions to me."

Evelyn couldn't understand why she freaked out when her husband tried to make love to her. He was sensitive and gentle. He was funny and attentive. The candles were lit. Music was playing. The room was just the right temperature. As he slipped off her beautiful negligee, she froze. All the little hairs stood up on the back of her neck. Her eyes shut tight. Her arms crossed over her chest and her ankles twisted around each other and gripped so tightly they left marks the next day. No sex tonight.

She was in the second year of therapy for bingeing and purging when she began to make sense of the situation. She couldn't understand why her husband hadn't left her. She knew that marriage was for better or for worse. This certainly was for worse. The therapist, Samantha Smith, thought she knew what was coming, but didn't assume anything until it emerged clearly. There was no suggesting of repressed memories. At one point during a family gathering when her stepbrother, Zeb, hugged her tightly, Evelyn began to make a connection between her distressed marriage and what had happened to her during those nights of being babysat by Zeb. He would give her a bath, taking a long, long time to be sure she was clean, and then he put her in bed, turned off the light, and got in beside her. She closed her eyes tightly and pretended to be asleep, but she could feel his fingers again, once more going where they shouldn't go. He kissed her on the mouth and many other places.

When she was about seven, even though she had gotten older, he was still so much bigger and stronger. She couldn't stop feeling him inside of her. He told her, "This is special between us. I know you want it, and I just can't say no to someone who asks so nicely. But this is only between us. But don't say a word about this to anyone, or I'll do to you what I did to that rag doll of yours." It was only after Zeb enlisted in the Army and left home when she was 11 that things stopped.

To Hip, a touch was a touch. He didn't have any eyes. He only had connections to Evelyn's skin and her hormones. He had learned a long time ago that any touch is bad. He had a direct road to Myg, who would send out all the troops whenever Hip gave the orders. Hip didn't know that Evelyn's husband's touch was a different touch from Zeb. Frolob, the frontal lobe leader, tried to get through, but there was no direct connection to Hip; Myg only responded to Hip. So, every time her husband caressed her, Hip went into action.

Hip: "I know that you need my help, Evelyn. I'm calling Myg into action. Go to it, Myg."

Finally, Dr. Samantha Smith was able to pave a new road between Frolob and Myg, and between Frolob and Hip. It took a lot of work to grow a new neural connection, but finally, with Frolob's firm but clear direction and a new tau blocker, Hip began to identify the difference between past stepbrother's touch and loving husband's touch.

Four years into their marriage, Evelyn was able to participate in, and sometimes even enjoy, sexual relations. She couldn't believe how good her husband was in being patient and understanding and in supporting her therapy. Not only was his touch okay, she learned to reach out to him and be a full partner. The leash on Myg was loosened whenever a stranger approached at a party. But finally Hip learned the importance of different kinds of touch, and Myg was able to respond only when Frolob gave the command, not Hip. Frolob's high cortisol gradually improved, and finally there was harmony within the brain. Frolob could now say:

Frolob: "Hip knows the difference between the two men. Myg is going to go be at your service until you and your husband both go over the top together. Then he'll go back to sleep. Enjoy. Be at peace."

Frolob, Hip, Myg, Evelyn, Dr. Smith, and the kind, caring, sexually exciting husband finally became a team working together, not in opposition.

Comment

The issue of the origin of bulimia nervosa is complex. The hypothesis that it is due to childhood sexual abuse, and especially repressed memory of childhood abuse, is controversial, and only true in selected cases. What is not helpful is therapists suggesting memories into the minds of patients. The problem with past abuse is more the difficulty in forgetting it than the inability to remember it. On some level of consciousness, past sexual abuse is always present.

Parts of the brain, however, are not connected to current events or to the reasoning of the frontal lobe. When a pattern of emergency reaction has been established in childhood, then the hippocampus develops an emergency response to any touch memory. It alerts the amygdala, which is more like a shotgun with a hair trigger than anything else. Since there are few direct connections between the parts of the brain that can process and reason about what's going on in the frontal lobe and the emergency response team of Myg and Hip, it is crucial for this primitive protection system to update itself. For some patients, a kind and loving touch leads to a fear response that is apparently generated only from past bad touch. Helping these patients to live in the present and not the past, and to make changes in their neural emergency response system, are vital to their experiencing caring, loving, and enjoyable sexual relationships. Clinical story true—the rest is my version of neural connections.

Originally published in 2000.

47

The Harried Mother and the
Perfect Poop Collector

perfectionism, quality of life

Once upon a time there were two young women, Harriet and Peg. Harriet was a harried mother with two kids and a messy home. As a single mother whose husband died as a test pilot, she learned to tolerate crumbs under the table until getting around to her once-a-week cleaning. Her philodendron survived but the fern did not. Plants were watered once a week if she remembered. The kid's TV hours were limited. Stories were read to them. Their torn jeans were not always mended, but they knew when they came in from playtime that there would be hot chocolate waiting for them. Those weeds in the garden never quite got pulled. The kids sometimes were less than thrilled about the limits on their behavior. However, they basked in the unquestioned love they received. Occasionally Harriet was late to picking them up in day care and ended up paying small fines. Although holiday gifts were modest, each one was selected with an eye toward what the kids enjoyed. Every other week she was able to put away a few dollars for their college education. She did not always feel in control of life but concentrated on the essentials. As for her makeup, the dab of lipstick occasionally failed to meet at the corners. As for eye shadow, forget it.

Peg by contrast never did anything that wasn't perfect. She was absolutely horrified at the mess that pigeons made with their poop. She made it her life's calling to be the perfect poop collector. She designed a scraper to clean up poop in any weather and made sure her neighborhood park never had poop uncollected. She perfected her technique to the point where she developed a patent for a "Scoop the Pigeon Poop Collector System." She went on to perfectly analyze pigeon poop for several countries. She soon became an expert at the seasons and rhythms of pigeon poop and collected samples in bottles labeled as to color, local diet, and degree of liquid content. She wrote letters to the editor about the need to free the world of pigeon poop: feed them a higher fiber diet, outfit each of them with diapers, and organize a bond drive to fund the project. Every day she went out for collections. Her makeup was immaculate. Her clothing was stylish. She thought about new and better ways to collect pigeon poop and developed labels for her devices in several languages. Her house was, of course, immaculate. The white furniture and rugs never showed a trace of dust. Twice a day cleaning made sure that no speck of dirt lingered long in her home. Her fern was luxurious from frequent misting. Her motto was: "Anything worth doing is worth doing perfectly."

Comment

Perfectionism is an integral part of the personality of many eating disordered patients, especially those with anorexia nervosa. Theories suggest that for some individuals the complexities of everyday life are overwhelming and strike terror at a perfectionist heart. Reducing weight, dieting, exercising obsessively, and seeing the numbers on the scale go down all can be done to a high degree of perfection. But for what purpose? Perfectionism is highly overrated, hard to define, and of vanishing significance in the long run. A better motto for these patients would be

"Anything worth doing is worth doing adequately."

Many times new activities are not tried because unless they can be done perfectly they are too scary to try. Except for flying large planes and doing neurosurgery, achieving adequate, reasonable goals is a much better guideline to living life in a happy and sane manner. Perfection also has many built-in negatives. The alternative to perfection is usually a sense of failure because of the all-or-none, black-and-white thinking. It's hard not to find somebody who's better at any given activity. When self-esteem depends on perfection, self-esteem is diminished rather than elevated. It's only when patients confront the ruthless, implacable, harsh demands of a perfectionistic conscience that they can obtain any rest, happiness, and sense of fulfillment.

Sometimes it helps to point out the ridiculousness of perfectly carrying out garbage, perfectly picking up the pet's poop, or perfectly chasing down every dust molecule. Achieving adequate goals is a much more satisfactory target for living. Harried Harriet can look back with satisfaction for having raised a couple of loving, less than perfect, but secure kids. What can Peg look back on? Help our patients to live thoroughly adequate lives without perfection, unless of course they are the pilot on the plane you're flying in or taking out your pituitary tumor. Rest in peace, perfectionism. Long live adequacy.

Originally published in 2000.

48

Clip and Clop

all ED, therapy

Clip and Clop were two horses, both veterans of the farm scene. They were so well trained that a plow could be harnessed behind them and they could be set free in a field of winter rye to be plowed under for crop growth for next spring. They were able to accomplish the task without their owner being present. She of course would harness them up, bring them to the entrance of the field, and set them on their way with a pat on the haunches and a cheery, "Go to it, Clip and Clop." As the farm owner walked back to her fall canning underway in the big country kitchen, Clip and Clop started off, making a straight furrow through the slick winter rye. Clip and Clop were very different in personality. Clip was a high-spirited, fawn colored horse, who loved nothing more than a good time. He knew just how to get that extra apple or carrot from a passerby who reached over the fence to give him a treat. When Clip saw a potential target coming, he would prance with his legs high, turn, smile as only a horse can do, and give a playful whinny. Clop, despite the congenital blindness in his left eye, was a steady, solid performer who knew what he had to do and did it with quiet goodwill but no show.

Clop could never understand why, when he had moved 100 feet

down the furrow, he suddenly felt the harness pulling heavily against his shoulders. But he was a dependable horse and pulled with all of his might, knowing that farmer Sally depended on them. As they were coming to the end of the furrow, the load seemed to get lighter, at which point he turned around and started back the other way to make a parallel furrow. Once again the load got extremely heavy after 100 feet. Clop could not understand why with good Iowa soil, and before the freeze, the job sometimes became so hard.

This process went on until the entire two acres were plowed and high noon arrived. Farmer Sally came out to see the horses and bring them back for their bucket of water and pail of mash. She looked at her two sturdy horses and said, "My goodness, Clop, you must be getting old, you are all sweaty even though the day is cool. You look like you have gone through the war. We may have to think about the glue factory." Then she turned to Clip and said, "Clip, you are every farmer's dream. Your head is high, you look like you have barely worked. There will be an extra treat for you today."

When neighboring farmers, Sam and Sara came over to visit that evening and to have a cup of farm coffee, they settled in for a game of poker with the fourth member, neighbor Lyle. Soon the hard work of the day was forgotten, and stories were told with hearty laughter from all.

"Why Sally, you have the smartest horse I have ever seen. That Clip is a real card; I would not want him at a poker game. If you see Clip wearing sunglasses and a visor hat, watch out, he will take you for everything you have."

Sally replied after a moment's thought. "Don't you mean Clop, the horse with one good eye who always pulls on the right side? He makes you feel he has been working so hard, but I think it is just show. He wants something extra. It is that Clip who is the dependable one.

"Well, Sally, take a look some morning when the two are working together and you will know what I mean."

Sally soon forgot about the comment in the flurry of chat and cards during the rest of the evening. The next morning, however, as she was letting the bread rise for the day's supper, she stepped outside to see what farmer Sam meant. *I think he has the two horses mixed up*, she thought. She quietly walked out and slipped behind the bushes on the boundary of the property until she could see the two horses plowing the winter rye. After the pair turned a corner and the furrow bit deeply, she could see Clop straining mightily while Clip went down on his front knees and coasted along the slick winter rye, being pulled by Clop who had bulging eyes and heaving chest. Towards the end of the furrow where they were coming close to make a turn, Clip jumped up, put his shoulder to the harness and the two of them easily made the turn. They then started down the next row until about 100 feet into the new furrow, when Clip went back down on his front and hind quarters, coasting along, swatting flies with glee. You could almost make out a smug smile. At the end of the day, farmer Sally greeted the two horses and led them back to the barn. This time she said, "Clip, I have got your number. Half a bucket of mash for you, no apple, and tomorrow you will be working on the right side of the team.

Comment

Treatment of eating disorders is not a drop off and get fixed procedure. Undoubtedly the patient's role in the treatment of appendicitis or a strep throat is somewhat meaningful but usually minimal, mostly following direction for medication or activities. With eating disorders, treatment really only works when there is a partnership between therapist and patient, with the healthy part of the patient and the trained part of the therapist working together to defeat the eating disorder, replacing it with healthy thinking and healthy patterns of behavior.

I am sure we have all had the experience of seeming to engage with a patient, sincerely and carefully talking over treatment plans, getting down to work, and then scratching our heads and wondering why it seems like we are doing all of the work ourselves. Of course, the patient will say they are working as hard as they can, and gee whiz, if the therapist would only give a little more care and try a bit harder, the eating disorder would go away. So back to work the therapist goes, challenging those cognitive distortions, doing role play for the birthday party coming up featuring Aunt Tilly's famous German chocolate cake. Then the Monday after the party, the patient says, "I just did not feel prepared, I really did not understand what you meant last week. I hope you are going to be able to help me more effectively this week." Suddenly the therapist realizes that he or she is doing virtually all the work while the patient is coasting. We are not talking about true resistance springing from challenging cognitive distortions and the illness-based identity, but a slick pattern of coasting with a strong component of being manipulative. It is hard to figure out whether to get angry, laugh, or do more therapeutic interpretation.

I find the best thing is to say—in a clear, help-oriented, gentle, and firm tone, "This therapy work is a lot like a team of horses pulling a furrow here in Iowa. It only works when the two of us put our shoulders to the harness and pull together. So I am going to challenge you right now and say to you, let's work together. Here is what I want you to do for homework tonight—document your mood and your thoughts in your journal. Then, at supper, follow your full food plan. 1 think you have developed a pattern of sweet talking your parents and now me into doing all the work. I wish you well. If you are really ready to do your part, let me know. If not, goodbye."

Try switching chairs and put the patient in the therapist chair with yourself in the patient chair and see what kind of role exchange you can have. Sometimes a "Farmer Sam" or other observing team member will give you feedback on what the patient is doing in the therapeutic community when they think they are unobserved. This is not a reason for scolding or blaming the patient but a time to challenge the patient. We want to do our parts but we can't contribute the energy of both patient and therapist. Unless the team pulls together, it is time to change the team.

Originally published in 2000.

49

The Mule and the Canyon

all ED, quality of life

What a splendid vista the Grand Canyon presents. Looking into the canyon at sunset, with its many subtle levels of color on the canyon walls, you will agree there is no grander sight in the world. Pete the mule, however, had a different point of view. He trudged up and down the narrow path to the Bright Angel plateau and the Canyon Ranch. He slowly descended each morning and then slowly trudged up in the late afternoon. His saddlebags were filled with precious water for the hikers who trekked down on their own and camped below. His water bags were somewhat leaky, however and they left a trail of drops all down the path. Also, every once in a while, his foot began to slip and he would knock a bit of vegetation off the side of the path and down the hillside, which was steep and desperately needed vegetation to hold onto the remaining soil. In addition, Pete left some droppings along the path, as all animals do. What goes in must come out. "What an uneventful life this is."

Pete was intermittently discouraged about his role in life. He really wanted to be a galloping stallion or a splendid racehorse. He envied the Austrian show horses he saw one day out of the corner of his eye on a television set. "What a donkey's life this is, being a mule. I can't even have little Petes." One day, after 20 years of service, Pete lay down in the stable, after a long hot day. He had eaten his oats and hay. He felt vaguely satisfied but also physically ill. Sure, he had given pleasure to many, but what had he done with his life except trudge up and down the path.

At the memorial service for Pete two days later, the young head mule gathered all the other pack mules together to hear a simple moving talk. "Let's remember the way Pete lived his life. This is an example for us. I know he felt that he was only a pack animal and not like the stallions and racehorses he admired. But everywhere Pete went, he left a trail of water that allowed rare cactus to grow. Whenever he kicked a bit of vegetation off the trail, it fell down and took root on the hillside. We now have a hillside lush with vegetation. And Pete's droppings were among the best. They gave nutrients to many small plants and starving saplings that now flourish. Let's give a hearty whinny for Pete. He did much good that he never appreciated. They also serve who do their jobs each day to the best of their ability." And they all gave a hearty whiney and went back to their hay.

Comment

Many people believe that they have to lead spectacular lives or gain recognition from others. By living a simple dedicated life, people often do much good without realizing it. Steadiness of purpose, consistency of effort, kindness to others, all leave long lasting impressions. Pete the mule did much good without realizing it. We all need the faith that by living our lives conscientiously much good is done that we'll never know about. This goes for housepainters who paint walls, for garbage collectors who clean our neighborhoods, and for therapists who see patient after patient. Let us salute quiet consistency and let others know they are appreciated before their memorial service.

Originally published in 2000.

50

Missy and Magical Thinking at the Party

all ED, cognitive distortion, magical thinking

Once upon a time there was a girl named Missy who was looking forward to the annual family party. It was that time of year when Spring was poking its head out from the defrosting ground along with the first daffodils and the new green grass. This was a real tradition for her family. Come one, come all to the party, all family members. When Missy started thinking about the party she thought to herself, "Aunt Tillie is going to do it again—she's going to tell me I've gained some weight." Well, that can't be helped. "And Uncle Jeb, I'm sure he's going to tell me that my dress is too short." But there's always Cousin Patsy though, she's usually a real faker. She'll look at me and say how nice I look, what perfect makeup I have on.

But Missy was looking forward to seeing Grandma Jones. She planned to say, "Grandma, great to see you again. Thanks so much for the birthday card." But as Missy began to think, she said to herself, "I know Grandma's going to get on me for my grades. I know she thinks that anything less than an A means I'm lazy." Nonetheless, Missy kept on driving to the party sure that her brother Joe would be decent. "Now that I think of Joe, I bet he's going to ask if I still have my thunder thighs."

By this time Missy was feeling hot under the collar. She tried deep breathing and thinking of a peaceful sunset over the water. The relaxation didn't last long because she knew Dad would rag on her for spending too much money for her new car. "I know that Mom is going to ask me why I'm not going with someone." When Missy got to the party she straightened her leather skirt, glanced in the car mirror, grabbed the lemon meringue pie she'd baked, and strode to the door with a head of steam. Once inside the door, the wonderful aroma of roasting chicken and spring flowers hit her. The table was beautifully set. There were Japanese lanterns hung from the beams with little candles inside. Background jazz was playing.

Aunt Tillie approached her to give her a hug but before she could hug Missy, Missy stepped back and glared at her. "If you're going to pick on my weight, you can just shut your mouth right now." Uncle Jeb was right behind Aunt Tillie. Missy reached for the lemon meringue pie and before Uncle Jeb could say anything she plastered him in the face with it. "Of all the nerve, telling me that my dress is too short. Everybody is wearing this today." Like a torpedo out a submarine, Missy moved on to cousin Patsy and gave her a slap saying she had some nerve criticizing Missy's makeup. As for Grandma Jones, all she got was, "You're a nice person, Grandma, but I'm sick and tired of you telling me my grades are not good enough." Brother Joe was put in his place with an abrupt comment, "Joe, don't even open your mouth. I know what you're going to say." As for Mom and Dad, all they heard as Missy left, before the door slammed, was "I'll settle down when I want to settle down, Mother. And Dad, it's my money not yours, so shut up."

The whole family was very confused and rattled by Missy's outburst. Aunt Tillie had been ready to give Missy a hug and tell her what a beautiful young girl she was. Uncle Jeb was about to tell her how gorgeous she looked. It took Uncle Jeb some time to get the lemon meringue pie off his face, shirt, jacket, and tie. Cousin Patsy always felt insecure around Missy because of how beautifully Missy applied her makeup. Grandma Jones was left dumfounded. Brother Joe first felt angry then sorry. Mom and Dad shook their heads and said, "You try your best, but sometimes you don't know how kids will turn out."

It took Missy several days to get over her anger, at all the rude things people were thinking about her, at their insensitivity, unkindness, and fake attempts at making pleasant comments. It was clear to her that she would never attend another family party.

Comment

This pattern of "magical thinking" or projection is fascinating. Many of our eating disorder patients mistake what they think other people think for reality. In their own minds, they create the script that others will speak and then how they must respond. It all feels so real. They're so sure that one person will say this and another person will say that. How sad that they never find out what other people think because they don't give them a chance.

A treatment goal of patients with self-doubt and social insecurity is to help them recognize when they're practicing magical thinking or projection. Let's teach them that they will never know what someone thinks until they say it clearly, or you ask them and they respond.

Originally published in 2000.

51

The Cork and the Buoy

recovery tool, all ED, impulsivity

The Cork and the Buoy were having a conversation one day in the New York Harbor. Cork said to Buoy, "You live such a restrictive life. Look at me. I'm free to go with the waves. Yesterday, I touched the tip of Manhattan and the day before I was at the Statue of Liberty. Why don't you loosen up and ride the waves."

Buoy said to Cork, "You're right, 1 can't do all the things you do. I'm not exactly immobile, however. You see I can move around in a pretty big circle and sometimes even get close to the Staten Island Ferry when it passes by. "

And so it went. Cork kept teasing the Buoy while it rode the waves, and Buoy remained securely grounded to the bottom of the harbor with its sturdy anchor. Everything went well until Hurricane Floyd swept over the area with its heavy rain and high tides. Cork couldn't resist teasing Buoy again. "Look at me. Look how free I am. I haven't had so much fun in a long time. I've been up on the top of the biggest waves ever and I've been down between the waves. You've got to get a life sometime."

Hurricane Floyd brought an enormous sprawling area of drenching rain, stretching several hundred miles from Maryland to Massachusetts. After a while Cork stopped teasing Buoy and started looking worried. "Hey Buoy, can I come over and visit?" Actually, Cork was getting scared. The waves were getting higher and higher. What used to be fun was no longer any fun.

Cork tried to maneuver itself over to the Buoy. For a while Cork was able to stay inside the circle of metal just below the blinking light of the red Buoy. Incidentally, this was a "red right return" Buoy guiding ships so they wouldn't run aground when entering the harbor.

After a while however, the rains increased even more. The tides became stronger and the waves ranged higher. Soon Cork was swept over the encircling metal band of the Buoy and moved helplessly toward the open ocean. After a while Buoy couldn't even see Cork. Buoy flashed its lights even faster than usual trying to help Cork see the way back, but to no avail.

Cork was swept out through the narrow channel connecting the upper and lower harbors and finally exited out past Coney Island into the Atlantic. At first Cork was nibbled on by a shark, which quickly spit him out. Then Cork was pierced by one of those floating hypodermic needles that a New York City addict had thrown into the harbor. Between the constant up and down of the waves and the pounding rain, plus nibbles from a few other sea creatures, Cork broke into many pieces and disappeared forever.

Comment

One day I was trying to explain to a patient why excessive emotional ups and downs lead to problems. The lack of a secure emotional grounding, and the intense emotional ups and downs were from my perspective a problem, not a source of restriction as she saw it. The analogy I used was the Cork and the Buoy—the contrast between the individual who is always emotionally up and down with no source of stability, versus the person anchored to solid emotional ground. It may be fun to ride the waves for a while but there is no personal control. Eventually you are at the mercy of the environment and the creatures in the environment. What seems to be a less exciting life, namely anchored to the harbor bottom with a reasonable but not unlimited range of movement, but never being out of control, is a good thing not a bad thing.

How to make a Cork into a Buoy is more complex and, of course, the analogy may crumble if pushed too far. But it gives the borderline patient, especially the very young borderline-in-the making, some insight into the difference between having an emotional anchor versus a lack of personal control. It's really no fun to be so ungrounded. But having emotional stability does not mean lack of capacity for emotional flexibility or response. It just means that when hurricanes, and sharks, and other dangerous objects, conditions, and creatures come, you'll probably survive the experience better and keep doing your job, sending out some light, if you are a Buoy and not a Cork.

Originally published in 2000.

52

Marguerite's Deal

thinness, weight prejudice, all ED

Once upon a time, in a kingdom long, long ago, there lived a young country girl named Marguerite. She had a happy childhood except for the occasional warnings from her mother that she should be careful and not become fat like her aunt. Upon turning 13, Marguerite noticed that she was developing hips, some roundness in her thighs and a feminine figure overall. These changes worried her. One day at sunset, while standing under a cherry tree, she pondered what to do about these changes in her body. She thought she saw a figure emerge in front of her but did not know if it was a shadow from the setting sun or a real person. Soon it became clear that it was a slim, mysterious woman of unknown age who had stepped out of the shadows. She wore a long black dress with slits up the sides. Her long curved fingernails were painted bright red. Her hair was jet black.

"Marguerite, my dear, you look so worried. What are you thinking about?"

Marguerite responded, "I don't know who you are, but maybe you can help me. I just turned 13. I don't like the way my body is developing. I'm worried about becoming fat like my aunt."

"Well, Marguerite, I have a deal for you. Lots of other girls have made the same arrangements. Trust me. If you will promise me that sometime far in the future, when you're very, very old, you'll come and live in my kingdom, I'll make sure that you're thin all your life. When you go to college and join a sorority, you won't be teased. You will have princes from the entire kingdom fighting for your hand. When you give birth to your darling children, you'll stay thin and sleek. When you become queen of the realm, you'll have the same figure you had when you were 12. You will wear the finest clothes and jewels. Give me your word that you'll come to my kingdom later."

Marguerite had to think about this a bit. Her mother had warned her not to talk to strangers. But it seemed like a reasonable deal. The future was so far off, and if she never had to gain weight, it would be worth it to make the deal. So she signed the little contract that the woman presented. She never really got her name, but the woman said she would come back from time to time to remind Marguerite of the deal.

It all came true. Marguerite went off to the best university and joined an elite sorority. All of her sorority sisters were dieting but Marguerite never had to do this. She could go to dances and the midnight supper afterwards, and eat what she pleased. Her sorority sisters were very envious.

Marguerite finally chose as her husband the Prince Svein of the most powerful kingdom. Prince Svein could not help giving her compliments every day about her beauty. When Prince Edward and Princess Sylvia came along, Marguerite stayed the same weight. Every few years she tried on her splendid wedding dress with its twenty-foot train, and was always able to fit into it without the slightest tightness. While Marguerite's women of the court gradually gained weight over the years, Marguerite confounded them all. Her figure stayed the same at age 17, at 24, at 35, and at the half-century mark.

At her diamond jubilee, when she turned 75 years old, the mysterious woman came to see Marguerite for the last time, having checked in every ten years or so to affirm that the deal was still in effect. But now the woman was there to settle the score. She said, "Tomorrow at sunset, you will follow me into my kingdom. You have lived a life of being thin, rich, and famous. Tomorrow at sunset I will meet you under the cherry tree and you will follow me."

The next day, as the sun was setting, Marguerite walked into the garden and stood under the cherry tree. There, the woman in the long black dress and the long red nails clasped Marguerite's hand and said, "Come. Follow me. It's time to go." Marguerite felt a sense of despair. She did not really want to go but knew she had to honor the deal.

Her husband, meanwhile, had noticed earlier that day that Marguerite was not her usual cheerful self. He asked her what was the matter and she brushed him off by saying, "Oh, nothing. I'm just tired." The King knew Marguerite well however and followed her when she went into the garden at sunset. They had always gone together at this time of day, so when she went alone, he knew something was up. When he saw the woman with the jet-black hair, the long black dress with slits up the side, and the long red nails, he instantly recognized that this was not a good person—especially when he saw the wicked glee on her face. She told the King: "Your wife has made a deal with me. I've allowed her to be thin all of her life when other women have put on weight and became well rounded. Now it's time for Marguerite to carry out her part of the deal. She must follow me to my kingdom."

The King responded, "You wicked woman. You are truly evil. I never cared if Marguerite was thin as a pencil, I love her for who she is, not for the size of her dress."

"Oh, Svein, I always thought you wouldn't love me if I put on weight like the other women. If I had known that you loved me for who I was, I would have never carried out this deal." At that moment, Svein jumped in between Marguerite and the wicked woman.

The woman drew her sword, "Out of my way. A deal is a deal."

Svein replied, "You will never take my wife to your kingdom. She belongs here with me." Svein then leaped toward the witch, letting her sword go through him. As he gasped his last breath, drops of blood fell on Marguerite's feet and she was magically transformed. Her figure filled out to become like the other women in her court of a similar age, pleasantly rounded, with glowing cheeks. She was even more lovely than when she was thin.

"Curse you, King Svein," said the woman in black, "You have broken the deal by the only means possible. When a noble man gives his life to save his wife, any deal with me is annulled. Even worse, you will revive from your wound and return to being King."

With a curse and a hiss, the wicked woman turned toward the sun. As she walked away, she disappeared into a gully where flames consumed her. Svein revived. He took one look at his now pleasingly normal wife and said, "Oh Marguerite, you look more beautiful than ever." The couple then lived on for the next 25 years in happiness and health. They passed a law forbidding anyone from ever commenting on a young girl's weight. The kingdom became happier and healthier.

Comment

The age-old story of the deal that Marguerite made with Faust is the source of operas, ballet, movies, and plays. It seems so tempting to make a deal with the current Faustian culture that will guarantee thinness, but for what purpose? So many young girls believe the illusion that they will be happy and loved only if they remain thin. Prince Svein had tried his best all of his married life not to tell his wife that he really would like it more if she were not so thin. He wanted her to feel just a bit warmer when they cuddled, but he was wise enough not to say anything. It all turned out happily at the end of this fantasy. Unfortunately, the deal that young people make with our society's relentless norms mandating thinness do not always turn out as well. The deal breaker for today's contemporary wicked agreement to artificial thinness has to come from awakening the healthy side within a girl, often in cooperation with a skilled therapist.

Originally published in 2000.

53

Johnny the Giant Waters the Land

all ED, recovery tool, quality of life

Johnny the Giant was a big, big giant. He was so huge that when he stood up, his head was in the clouds. Not only that, but one foot was in Yesterday and the other was in Tomorrow. Now, Johnny loved diet colas. He couldn't get enough diet colas from the 24-hour convenience store called Pop's Instant Stop Shop. Johnny had another problem. He wanted to be smaller so he could date normal sized young woman. He figured if he drank enough diet colas, he could reduce his weight and be more attractive, less intimidating to a girl he might meet.

Johnny was also a restless giant, moving from one leg to the other. When he placed his weight on the left foot, standing in Yesterday, he thought of all the things he didn't do and felt guilty and sad. He thought about forgetting to pick the peas and beans for the canning company. He worried about leaving the tassels on the corn that should have been de-tasseled by now. He really put himself down for not brushing his teeth like Dr. Dent-de-Lion taught him to do. Despite these worries, the land of Yesterday was green and fertile, lush, and beautiful. He couldn't see that however.

As he fussed about Yesterday, he moved his weight to his right leg, and stood in Tomorrow. This was a land of a different kind of worry—filled with all the things that might go wrong. There was the husking of the corn that would be backbreaking. His great-uncle Siegemund might ask him once again to move the family mountain to the south for winter so great-uncle could get more sun during the cold months. That job was always a tough one, and he never did it fast enough. Plus, there would be the family reunion when everyone would tell him he was eating too much. Actually, Tomorrow looked pretty good to other people, with golden colors all over the land, but Johnny didn't see it that way.

As a result, he kept shifting his weight back and forth from one leg to another, from Yesterday to Tomorrow. And you know what happens when you keep drinking diet colas. What goes in must go out. Johnny kept buying more and more diet colas from Pop's Instant Stop Shop, and really needed to empty his bladder, which was situated right above the land called Today, which is where his steady stream fell. Too much liquid is just as bad for plants as too little; and, after all, plants can only take so much ammonia and electrolytes. But Johnny kept shifting his weight from Yesterday to Tomorrow, and he kept drinking diet colas. All those things he didn't do right yesterday, all those things that he might not be able to handle tomorrow. And soon Today was a sodden mass of withered plants that never got tended and gradually died, leaving Today as a barren wasteland.

Comment

While it's not a very elegant phrase, the truth is that when you keep one foot in yesterday and one foot in tomorrow, you piss on today. The here and now is the only place we can do anything, the only place where patients can make critical changes in their eating disordered lives. Now is the only time that change can be made, that growing encounters can be experienced, joy can be felt, love can be expressed, and dysfunctional ways of thinking can be corrected. How often do patients keep shifting from guilt about yesterday to anxieties about tomorrow. Except for honest practical planning about the future and therapeutic review of the past in sessions, let's help our patients to focus on Here and Now—the only time and place that life can be lived. A day given over to shifting from the past to the future and ignoring the present is a day that is pissed on. Inelegant, yes, but true.

Originally published in 2001.

54

Saving the World from Prejudice

weight prejudice

Buffy and Muffy were walking out from their meeting on equal opportunity for women in investment firms. They agreed there is nothing so prejudicial as a woman working as hard as a man and not getting equal compensation.

"Muffy, didn't you think that representative from the Securities and Exchange Commission was fantastically on target with her points. Let's write our congressional representatives today to get legislation going. And, by the way, did you see how fat she was. If I were her, presenting before this group of powerful women, I'd do something about my weight. She must have been a size 16."

The dynamic pair moved on after a brief lunch of salad and miso soup to their next meeting with an advocacy group to stop prejudicial treatment of children with disabilities. There were so many important changes to make in the school system and to create opportunities for work as summer interns with legislators. The inconsistency of legislators made them boiling mad—the very group that passed laws to ensure fairness often did not practice those principles themselves. They were determined, and when Muffy and Buffy were determined, things happened.

The meeting was a big success, with promises made before the media for legislators to include disabled young people as interns.

"Representative Smith was totally sincere. I really believe him. Wouldn't he be perfect as a presidential candidate if he didn't have that gut and double chin. He must not have as much willpower as I thought he did," said Muffy. "It's a shame when people go to pot. Let's not let that happen to ourselves," she said as she smoothed an imaginary wrinkle from her size 3 Armani skirted suit. The world had too many prejudices for Muffy and Buffy to stop their day's work during supper. They planned the evening's strategy session on stopping public prejudice against AIDS victims while they quickly ate a small portion of broiled filet of sole and shared a dinner salad with just a squeeze of lemon juice as dressing.

"Oh, gross, Buffy. Do you see that woman over there? I couldn't help but notice that she had a hollandaise sauce on her broccoli and ate all of her chicken Kiev, which was stuffed with fat. And she ordered the crepes with a double serving of ice cream and chocolate sauce. She can't even pull herself all the way into the table. Her husband is just as bad. Somebody needs to get them off their fat butts and to the gym."

The meeting that evening went well. By the time Muffy and Buffy finished their convincing presentations, everyone in the room had made a personal commitment to root prejudice out of their hearts and daily behaviors. Many people commented on how Muffy and Buffy were the most sincere and prejudice-free people they had ever met. The two friends could not help but feel satisfied at the end of the day as they stuffed envelopes for the "Respect Native American Heritage" drive. Somehow they had to get Congressional approval to remove from public availability all those old Western movies with such prejudicial depictions of Native Americans.

"Hey, Muffy, I have an idea. Let's try to get a segment on the early evening news. That will reach more people than a town hall meeting. And, have you noted that Jessica Jones, the evening news anchor is putting on weight. She used to be so pretty. Now that she's had a child, she doesn't have those cheekbones any more. Her make-up hides the weight a little, but you can tell she is letting herself go. I think they need to replace her soon. But let's be polite and pretend we don't notice. After all, we have an important mission—we're here to make this society prejudice free."

Comment

Certainly, weight prejudice is in strong contention for a medal in the dubious race for the most severe lingering prejudice. Larger-than-average individuals are stereotyped to be weak-willed, self-indulgent, lazy, disgusting, and unattractive. Negative attitudes and prejudicial behaviors are commonplace and disastrous for children. Cruel words often last a lifetime when addressed to heavy children, and may be the seed for future eating disorders. Studies from the Cooper Clinic in Texas show that fitness is the most important factor in health, not weight (except, perhaps in cases of morbid obesity). Let's relate to people as individuals with unique personalities, and potential for friendship, not as depersonalized objects relegated to a category of "fat" people. Remember the shrewd teaching from the New Testament: remove the two-by-four timber from your own eye before you try to remove the speck of dust from someone else's.

Originally published in 2001.

55

Three Campers

all ED, causes for ED

Once upon a time, Tom, Dick, and Harry signed up for a wilderness survival course. They each had grown up in Brooklyn, living their lives on concrete. They knew where to get the perfect egg cream, and the absolute best storefront pizza. They knew very little about where milk came from, whether corn grew on trees or bushes, or how to survive outside of a big city. This wilderness survival camp would teach them.

The final test, after two weeks of preparation, was to enter a forest several miles from each other and spend a full 36 hours without equipment or assistance from anybody else. They were brought to their individual starting locations with blindfolds on, so they had no idea where they were; and, the only directions they had were to walk 100 paces into the forest without looking back.

Tom was left at a forest edge with lush vegetation, lots of dry twigs, and berries galore. After a couple of hours of hiking, he found a stream, scooped up water in his palms and drank until he was satisfied. He thought maybe the forest cuisine was leaner than a good *pierogi*, but with some berries and water, he would make it through. Now all he had to do was light a fire and rest for the night. He gathered twigs and leaves, dried branches, and fallen pine needles. "This should not only keep me warm, it should smell good—just like the Christmas trees we burn in the neighborhood." He looked around for a couple of rocks to strike against each other to get a good spark going, but after a half hour, then an hour, then two hours, he found absolutely nothing with which to start a fire. It was a long, cold night, but he survived buried in the leaves and he hiked out the next afternoon in not particularly good spirits.

Dick bounded into his part of the forest—an area recently swept clean by an avalanche and then some torrential rains. After hiking to the top of the hill, he immediately saw some flint-like stones and knew he was in luck. Making a fire would be a cinch for him. Soon night came, and Dick began to worry. He set off lots of sparks from the flint, but he could find absolutely no vegetation to light, except tender green shoots which were moist and completely nonflammable. He had a difficult time finding a place to hunker down, but he managed with green twigs as bedding and slept a fitful night. He was cross and chilled when he made his way back the next afternoon to the starting point.

Harry at first was confused about what to do, but soon gathered his wits and began finding bits of kindling as the afternoon sun started to set. He gathered a nice mix of dry twigs with leaves underneath. As luck would have it, he found a couple of stones that produced sparks quickly. Soon Harry was roasting the fish he caught in the stream, then nestled himself snugly in his cocoon of pine branches and stayed reasonably comfortable throughout the night.

The evening after completing their survival test, they agreed that city kids belong in the city. Country kids can keep the outdoor adventures all to themselves. At least in the city you could light a newspaper with a match, not search for twigs and flintstones

Comment

Eating disorders can be thought of as syndromes that "light and burn" when there is a combination of predisposition plus precipitation.

These long words are not very communicative to young people who have not been immersed in medical and psychological jargon. What they often respond to is the idea that eating disorders "catch" when there is both kindling and a spark. You can have all the kindling in the world, such as being a young girl, in a suburban household, with a perfectionistic temperament, who takes ballet, and has a family history of depression. But if there is no spark, such as a rude weight comment or a peer urging her to diet, then the predisposition (kindling) won't light. Even gasoline won't blaze without a spark.

The opposite situation occurs when there is no significant predisposition or kindling but plenty of sparks. If, for example, you take an extroverted personality, perhaps an inner city guy, or a young woman growing up in a loving, communicative, extended family with meaningful connections, then all the media-based dieting articles in the world, all the comments from rude strangers or acquaintances about fatness, even participation in wrestling or gymnastics, won't cause a blaze to occur— because there is no kindling to light.

But when you put the two together, as with Harry, the more the kindling and the more intense the spark, the more likely a fire will occur and the longer it will burn.

Originally published in 2001.

56

Life on the Peak of the Roof

all ED, cognitive distortion, recovery tool, black & white thinking

Ivan, a roofer in 19th Century Russia, was always clinging to one side of the roof or the other. He would try to do his work on one side and then he would move gradually up to the peak of the roof, sit there for a while, and then slide down the other side, barely catching himself before falling off. He did this day after day, month after month, year after year. Life was very hard for Ivan. He could never stand up straight. He could barely hold on. He was always afraid that he would fall off one side or the other. One night, Ivan dreamed that Tevya, a musician playing a fiddle, was walking on a flat roof with a big house underneath. He confidently moved along playing old Russian folk tunes on his fiddle, and didn't worry at all about falling. Ivan dreamed he could be like this musician and that he didn't have to bend over to stay balanced.

The next day, Ivan decided to only work on flat roofs of houses, where he could stand straight up, do his work without bending over, and not be afraid of falling. Thanks to the dream of Tevya, soon Ivan was a much happier man and more successful in his work.

Comment

Many patients think that the moment they are no longer starving themselves they are fat. This pattern of thinking is often called "black and white thinking" or "all or none reasoning." These patients act as if they're poised precariously on one slope, the starvation slope, with the only option being to flip to the other side of the roof where they're in danger of obesity.

I ask patients to imagine that, instead of staying on the slope of starvation or sliding down the slope of obesity, they should imagine a large flat picnic ground with a cliff at one far end and a cliff farther than they can see at the other end. The level ground is the broad normal range in which we want all patients to enjoy their picnic of life. I tell them that their bodies will let them know which part of the broad normal range they belong in after they have adjusted to healthy eating and exercise.

The visual image reinforces the idea that you can't go from starvation to obesity without passing through this plateau of a broad normal range. The comparison between life on the slope of a peak roof and life on a large flat picnic ground has very different emotional and cognitive consequences. While it's helpful to identify a cognitive distortion, I think that substituting a healthy image in its place is a good way to present a positive, emotionally healthy image.

Originally published in 2001.

57

Frank the Fish Takes the Bait

teasing, therapy

Frank was a fish with a very puffy, torn lip. Poor Frank! He could never pass by a baited hook. Even when the barb was poking through, all he could think of was that luscious worm. The wriggling night crawler made his juices flow.

He remembered what his father had said, "Don't take bait. Never take bait. Look for that barb." Nonetheless, Frank jumped at the hook each time. He might be swimming away in the opposite direction, but just a little glimpse of a minnow dangling in the water would cause him to turn around and take the bait.

The piscine emergency room groaned when they saw Frank coming again. His lip was so shredded from taking the bait that there was little tissue left for a repair. No matter how many times this happened, a hook with bait was an invitation he could not turn down.

Whoosh! Whoosh! There goes Frank taking the bait again.

Comment

Every time a person responds defensively—with anger, fear, or humiliation—to a "barbed" comment by someone else, they are just like

Frank the Fish—they are taking bait. We see this in kids all the time. Mike tells Art that he's a skinny wimp and Art starts throwing things while Mike laughs. Art took the bait. Art in turn tells Liz that she is fat. She cries and goes to the mirror to look at herself. Liz took the verbal bait.

Every kid knows how to get his sibling or school chum to turn red in the face. To find the vulnerable spot, offer them verbal bait. All kids know how.

Let's help young people to recognize that verbal bait always has a hook in it and their lip—or, more likely, their self-esteem—will suffer. If they take the bait, it's a losing situation. When you find a patient whose life is made miserable by responding to verbal negativity, help him or her to recognize and label the verbal put-down as bait. Ask if they really want to take bait and be like Frank the Fish.

Once patients recognize that this is not in their best interest, they can learn by role playing some brisk, assertive answers. Some of the phrases I find helpful to teach them are: "Thanks, but I don't take bait," "Quit talking to yourself," and "It's a free country, and you're free to be wrong." Smart kids feel good enough about who they are and become savvy enough not to take bait.

Originally published in 2001.

58

Skeletons at the Dance

anorexia nervosa, loss of individuality, thinness

A bunch of skeletons got together for their annual dance. Skeleton Sue walked up to Skeleton Sarah and said, "I love that collar bone. I've never seen one so pretty."

In return, Sarah said, "And that forearm bone, Sue, it's so unique. You look so terrific without all that fat."

Sue was glad that her specialness of having the thinnest forearm bone was obvious. Sarah didn't mind showing off her collarbone either. Of course, their bones clinked a little when they walked along the dance floor edge.

Soon, Sissy, Sam, Seth, and Silky arrived and started dancing. Each one knew in his or her heart (really in their sternum since there was no heart left) that they were absolutely the most individual and special person at the dance. Each of them was sure he or she were the thinnest.

Suddenly the mood of the event darkened. In walked Jerry and Janet. Jerry was 6'1" and weighed 180 pounds, mostly muscle. He had on a gray suit with a black collarless shirt. Janet was 5'4" and weighed 130 pounds, and wore an elegant black pants suit with an old broach from her great-grandmother.

All the skeletons turned at the same time toward Jerry and Janet and said in unison, "Oh, get them out of here. Who would want to be like them? We're so special. They don't belong here. They're so ordinary. Poor them."

Jerry turned to Janet and said, "They're right, we don't belong. Let's get out of here. By the way, I can't figure out who is who at this dance. They all look alike. You know, one skeleton looks like another skeleton."

Comment

Many anorexia nervosa patients fear that if they give up their disease they will lose their special uniqueness. They say with great conviction they're special only when they're starved. They don't want to be "just another normal weight person" and lose their identity.

This belief is exactly 180 degrees wrong. Each starved patient looks very much like every other starved patient. They are bony, with sunken eyes, with little emotional expression. They look cold and pale. It is critical in therapy to convince anorexia nervosa patients that starvation causes them to lose all of their specialness and individuality. A starved person looks like a starved person—whether the result of anorexia nervosa, third world malnutrition, or being a political prisoner. Those terrifying photos of Nazi prisoners taken after WWII ended showed a group of emaciated human beings all looking exactly alike. All individuality was lost under the terrifying conditions of starvation.

If we can persuade patients with anorexia nervosa that starvation produces a loss of individuality, then we are making real progress. Maybe my old aunt wasn't so far off when she said, "God made one of you and then broke the mold."

Originally published in 2001.

59

Savannah's Rule

anorexia nervosa, thinness, cognitive distortion

Savannah was a smart attractive teenager with anorexia nervosa. She would be on her way to an exciting fulfilling life if it were not for her anorexia nervosa and Savannah's Rule.

Savannah's Rule was very interesting. Basically this rule said that other people's rules and principles applied to everyone else, but not to her. It was like apples fell upward from the apple tree in her yard, not down, like in other people's yards. More importantly, even though Savannah liked others because they were friendly, interesting, and caring, she believed she could only be liked by being thin.

Other girls at her same height and low weight were obviously medically starved. But Savannah, knew she looked healthy at this height and weight. When other people had a breakfast of eggs, cereal, and fruit, they were eating normally, but if she ate the same breakfast, she would be pigging out.

Other people would freeze in the winter, but Savannah would be hot. For most people, 2 plus 2 would be 4, but for Savannah 2 and 2 would be 5. Cars would move on a green light but Savannah would move on red. If obviously true rules of science and society that apply to everybody else don't apply to you, you're following Savannah's rules.

Comment

I have never met an eating disordered patient who would reject another person who was truly friendly, caring, and interesting because of that person's weight. But of course, the eating disordered person is sure that no one else would like them if they weren't thin. Why the double set of rules? Why this exception to the laws of social interaction and physics?

Perhaps Savannah's Rule is kept in place because to let go of it would mean dismantling the fundamental (although nonpsychotic) belief at the core of eating disorders: I am acceptable, liked, attractive, safe, in control, only when I am thin. The challenge of therapy for patients with anorexia nervosa is to dismantle this belief system that thinness is an essential requirement for survival, without producing hopelessness or demoralization.

This is where groups are very effective. While a patient can discount what a therapist says, it's much harder to discount the direct confrontation by other members of a group. For example, they may say to a new patient who is following Savannah's Rule, "Oh yeah, you're not thin, you're normal—everybody has bones sticking out like you do." In our groups, they say to each other, "You know, you're following Savannah's Rule again." After a combination of confrontation by the group plus therapy sessions in which this double standard is challenged, patients realize that maybe they are starved, and people could like them at a normal weight—for who they are, because in fact, they are interesting, likeable, and caring. To believe in themselves and to recover, eating disordered patients need to dismantle Savannah's Rule.

Originally published in 2001.

60

A Meeting of Senior and Junior Devils

all ED, weight obsession, thinness, scales, mirrors

A crisis had developed in the Council of Devils. The human scene was not at all going according to their plans. The human race was making progress. People were too happy. Something had to be done about this dire situation. No letting the angels get the upper hand. The Senior Devil put it plainly, "We have to do something right away. I want the three new Junior Devils to show their stuff and come up with a plan right away. If this current Earth situation of too many happy people is not corrected, we will go out of business. Give me a plan for making humans miserable."

Junior Devil #1 thought for a while and then came up with a brilliant plan. "Let's make a new machine called a scale. We will advertise this new devilish instrument widely and make every person conscious of their weight. We will teach doctors that everyone has to be below average. We will get teachers to weigh each student in front of the class and tease them, especially those sweet girls. We will make each of them miserable just when life should be fun, when they become young women in their

172

teenage years. I can't wait to see them suffer." Sure enough, within a few months of widely promoting the "war on obesity," girls and women, boys and men were weighing themselves obsessively and dieting with the hope of seeing the number on the scale go down.

Junior Devil #2 was insanely jealous of Junior Devil #1. He had to come up with a better plan, and sure enough, he developed another way to make people miserable. "Senior Devil, listen to me. I have a terrific idea. We will install mirrors everywhere. They'll fill entire walls in elevators, gyms, rest rooms, restaurants, homes, and schools. We will make it impossible for a person to walk down the street without stopping at a mirror and feeling disappointed. Because of all those pictures of starved 'clothes hangers' that we sneak into magazines, everyone will think that they look like a hunk of lard compared to the models. And, get this, we will curve some of the mirrors, especially in women's rest rooms and women's gyms, so that women look even bigger than they are." Within a month a new wave of misery swept over the Earth. This time guys got into the scene. They looked at the mirror and saw how flabby they were. They started taking steroids and working out insanely. Junior Devil #2 had succeeded.

Junior Devil #3 was desperate. How could he prove himself superior to his peers? He thought and thought. He consulted books on spells and curses. He peered up with his sulfurscope and saw several islands in the South Pacific, several counties in the rural areas of Canada, and cultural groups in northern Scandinavia that were composed of happy people. And you know what, none of these groups had television. His eyes gleamed with devilish glee. "Senior Devil, give me a chance. I will swoop into their homes while they sleep and install cablevision. More than that, I will make sure they all get Baywatch, MTV, every soap opera, and weight loss infomercials. Heh, heh, heh. Their happiness will vanish like a snowball in Hades."

It took more than a month, more than three months, but by the end of six months, the last happy folk had become miserable. The previously happy and well-adjusted families were bitterly divided by contests for who could become thinnest and most buff. The palm trees on the South Sea Islands all carried neon signs advertising weight loss centers. The reindeer in northern Scandinavia had notices around their neck about where to buy diet foods. People in the rural Canadian counties lost so much weight that the average citizen no longer needed snowshoes when it snowed—they were so light, they could walk even on soft snow and not fall down.

At last the Senior and Junior Devils could take a break and turn up the steam heat to maximum. They deserved to celebrate and congratulate each other. They had now made each human being miserable in one way or another.

Comment

'nuff said.

Originally published in 2001.

61

Radar On-Line

abusive relationships, bulimia, magical thinking

Ann was excited about her wedding. Even though she was only 18, getting married would be a relief from living at her home. She had spent too much of her life with an alcoholic father and bitter mother. When she met Kirk, she found him dashing, romantic, and a lover of fast cars. He was not afraid to belt back a few drinks, but he could hold them and always treated her properly. She was sure that her secret bingeing and purging would stop when she got married. She had dieted down to a size 4 to get into a very special wedding dress. Finally the big day came.

Everything went well for the few months of their marriage, but Ann didn't like that their sex life was steadily diminishing. It seemed that after a night out with the boys, Kirk would come home with that unpleasant smell of whiskey and no interest in marital relations. When he got the DUI and was having trouble at work, she tried to be supportive. When she was pregnant in the second year of marriage, she was disappointed that he wasn't more excited. It was during their third year, when she was pregnant the second time, that she found motel receipts in his pocket, some lipstick on his collar, and a white powder in a zip-locked bag. She finally filed for divorce.

After each pregnancy, Ann restricted her food intake to get rid of the extra weight, but soon the binges and purges came back with a vengeance. At that time, she didn't even consider quitting the bulimia, because it seemed like the only way to get through the pressures of being a single parent and dealing with a difficult ex.

When she was about 23 and found a neighborhood girl to baby-sit, she took dance classes at the Y. She enjoyed feeling that sensation of being alive again—doing the three-step swing when the music was not too fast, and then going to the one-step for the up-tempo Lindy. "This is just like being on *Happy Days*. It is great to be free and to get a new start."

It was at the second dance that she noticed Brad. He was refreshing. He didn't seem to be overly impressed with himself even though he had a good job, one that took him out of town as a vice president at his company. When she danced with him, she felt secure and hopeful again. She was a little surprised by how quickly he proposed, only three months after they met. She thought to herself that here is a guy who can be trusted. He will make a good father. He loves the kids and wants to adopt them right away.

She could not believe her bad luck when Brad kept extending his out-of-town work assignments during their first year of marriage. After all, she was pregnant with their child. On the night of their first anniversary, Ann stayed home, bingeing and purging. When Brad finally got home around 2 a.m., with a long cut on his cheek and a bad bruise on his jaw, she patched him up and gave him a bag of ice to keep down the swelling. She was startled that he could have gotten into a steet fight, but she could not understand why he hadn't come home earlier or at least called for their anniversary. The next night she got another shock when a woman called asking for Brad and then quickly hung up. Suspicious, Ann reviewed the activity in their joint account, she realized only half of his paycheck was being deposited. When she confronted him, he tried to slime out of the truth, to no avail. After sobbing for a few days, having brought the children to her widowed mother, Ann got her act together and filed for divorce.

She waited five years, determined not to let bad luck happen again. She met Zeke at the bowling alley. Here finally was a guy who was stable. They had been bowling together on a team from work, so she was really getting to know him well. There was no question that Zeke was the only one for her. He was quick witted and made everyone feel good. When the season ended, they went out on a real date, and before long they were a couple. Her bad luck days were over and life would begin again. After all, many women don't settle down until their 30s.

This was like a bad dream, she thought less than a year later. He's just as screwed up as her other husbands had been.... It took ten years of being single, bingeing and purging the whole time, before there was hope again in her life. She knew that Fred was the one. She smiled when she had the thought, *bad news comes in threes*. This was a new start. She knew that Fred would be the right guy for her.

Comment

It is amazing how some people consistently select a partner who is exactly the wrong mate for them. It is almost as if they have radar. Actually, some patients with eating disorders seem to have a funny kind of radar. They can find the right "wrong" person mixed in with dozens of others. I don't know if it is caused by pheromones, brain signals, subtle messages from childhood, or what, but it is uncanny. The smart ones get clued in and realize there is something about the people they are first attracted to that is bad for them. They start finding that those other, seemingly uninteresting guys are in fact pretty neat if you give them a chance. The not-so-smart ones keep going through life being sure they are simply unlucky and fate has destined them for lousy relationships with bad guys (or gals). Let's help people to find good partners by changing the settings on their radar.

Originally published in 2002.

62

Catching Flashy Things

all ED, cognitive behavioral therapy, automatic thinking

Ickey and Pycey were talking during their daily trek to the brook in the woods. Each summer day, they went fishing and were determined at last to locate the source of the flashing things in the water that intrigued them every visit.

"Ickey, I am going to catch that flashing silver streak at last—you know, the one that looks like my silver bracelet when the sun hits it."

"Okay, Pycey, but I'm going for the creature that keeps stirring up the mud but always gets back under the rock before I can catch it." So off to the brook they went—no Red Riding Hood, no Big Bad Wolf, no toxic dumps, just a fun day in the woods for two kids with determination.

When they got there, they rushed up to the brook and saw the flashing silver in the water and the mud-stirring creature. Without hesitation, they plunged their hands into the water, but no luck. "Ickey, this won't work. We're too impatient. Let's step back awhile and let the water clear. Then we'll try again."

"You're right, Pycey."

So they retreated a few feet into the shade and watched quietly while the water cleared. Sure enough, soon the silver flashing resumed. Ever so slowly, Pycey crept up to the brook. She saw the rhythm of the silver flash, and at the right moment, quickly and cleanly put her hand into the water, bringing out a beautiful, bright fish. She carefully placed it in her clear plastic bucket and looked intently at the source of the elegant silver streak. What a beautiful fish it was: silver horizontal stripes, bright red eyes, and scales that refracted the sunlight into the colors of the rainbow. "Ickey, it wouldn't be right to take this fish home. It belongs in the brook. I'm going to put it back, but I'll never forget it."

Following her example, Ickey took his turn and inched up to the brook. He darted his hand like a laser into the water and scooped up a crayfish—at least for a moment, until it nipped his finger and he let it fall back into the water. "At least I saw what it was like, Pycey. It's a mean creature, but I respect its power. Did you see its pincer?!"

That evening, around the campfire with their friends, eating charred hot dogs and toasting s'mores, they tried to describe what it was like to finally catch the elusive creatures in the brook—the flashing thing, the mud-stirring creature. Of course, they embellished the story a little, but it was clear from their adventure that, with patience, even quick, nimble stream-dwellers could be caught long enough to see what they were really like.

Comment

One of the core techniques in Cognitive Behavioral Therapy is "catching" automatic thoughts and seeing what they are really like. These furtive creatures often provoke otherwise unexplained moods and behaviors. To identify an automatic thought, it is necessary for patients to slow down their relentless eating-disordered thinking and behaviors, to step back and become observers of the silver flashes or mud-stirrers, and then to capture them. Some of the thoughts are brilliant aspirations and dreams that can only be accomplished when the eating disorder energy is redirected into accomplishing healthy life goals. Some of the thoughts are disturbing—they might nip the narcissism of the perfection-ist, or disclose some id drives that had been covered over with intellec-tualization. But whatever they are like, they need to be patiently sought out, identified, and then let go back into the stream of the mind, but now with a genus and a species designation.

Originally published in 2002.

63

Anita and the Troll

anorexia nervosa, sexual abuse, thinness

Anita lived high up in the mountains with her family, several dozen chickens, and a goat. Once a week starting when she was seven years old, her mother sent her to market to sell the eggs and goat cheese in order to buy flour, beef bones, and dried fish in exchange.

To get to town Anita had to cross a bridge over a stream with a dark cavern under the nearside bank. The wooden slats on the bridge were so steep that Anita had to hold onto the slats with her hand. When she was about nine years old something happened that was very different as she crossed the bridge. A scaly hand reached up and felt her fingers as she made her way across the steep bridge. Suddenly the hand reached up and pulled her down into the cavern where the troll had his way with her.

Anita came back to her home a little later than usual, but mother didn't notice anything was wrong. Perhaps Anita appeared a little bit frightened the next time she was sent to the market, but she was compliant and went anyway.

After several more encounters with the troll, each time leaving her more and more frightened but feeling helpless about what to do, Anita hit on an idea: She would lose more and more weight and when the troll started to feel that her plump finger had become bony, maybe he would be less interested. Of course she said nothing to her mother about this but dressed in extra layers of clothing to hide her weight loss.

Sure enough the day came when the troll felt her finger on the bridge and instead of pulling her down pushed her away with an expression of disgust. He snorted and said, "I don't want any scrawny, bony creature down in my lair." Anita never told anyone about her encounters with the troll or why she became so thin. She turned down offers from Eric and Leif to go to dances and never married.

Until she was an old hunchbacked woman, she continued to cross the troll bridge each week to go to market, except for the Saturday after Christmas when she allowed herself to eat traditional cookies and stay home. But after that yearly reprieve, she was back to crossing the bridge with her bony fingers, as usual. She made sure her nieces and grandnieces never used the wooden slat bridge, but she would never tell them the reason why. She made sure they took a longer but safer way to market. "Poor Tante Anita," said one of her nieces, "they say she was so attractive as a young girl. I have no idea why she stayed so bony and scrawny, when she could have been beautiful."

Comment

Victims of sexual abuse are at risk for developing an eating disorder. As the result of instances of abuse, some sufferers make an association between their mistreatment and having an attractive body. The idea comes to the individual that maybe they would be safe from future attack if only they were thin, bony, and unattractive.

Lots of times, this association only surfaces after deep engagement in therapy, especially in cases where the girl or woman (and males, too) cannot get the event out of their minds but will not confide it to anyone else. She may act as if the assault never happened, but the trauma interferes with her ability to develop normal healthy sexual attitudes and desires—even with a caring partner.

Sometimes a hint comes when the patient's partner reports excessive anxiety around sexual relations or shuns affectionate expressions of love, when there is no apparent reason for the anxiety. Shame at disrobing and avoidance of contact with situations that harken even symbolically back to her previous assault may have a dramatic negative affect on a relationship.

All therapists must be cautious to not induce "false memories," but usually it is harder to forget experiences of sexual abuse than to remember them.

Originally published in 2002.

64

Maryland Thin

thinness, weight loss, cigarettes

Mary was named for Maryland, the state in which she grew up. She had a rich tradition, with ancestors dating back to the first settlers. Maryland, after all, was a distinguished state with a strong cultural and religious tradition. Maryland produced some of the best tobacco in the colonial days.

When Mary was 14, she began to notice that her hips were filling out. She didn't think that she could get into that size 6 dress any more, and with the junior prom coming up, having been invited by Todd, she wanted to look thin. She found Susie at first reluctant, but then by pleading with her, Susie gave her a few Maryland Thin cigarettes. She had heard that a half a pack a day would keep appetite under control and, even better, a full pack would allow her to stay on a reducing diet.

Mary didn't like inhaling the bus-exhaust-like fumes, but eventually tolerated them and enjoyed the buzz from the nicotine. It was true. She was able to skip breakfast, have a salad for lunch, and not do her usual afternoon binge. Well, maybe once in a while, but that was usually when she couldn't get her older friends to go into the convenience store for ciggies. Their IDs were fake, but at least they looked 18. There was no way anybody could mistake Mary for more than 14.

Mary and Todd had a great time at the dance. He told her many times how beautiful she was, how her dress fit her just right, and how glad he was that she wasn't "fat" like some of the other girls in her class. "If there's anything I want in a girl, it's a girl who knows how to take care of herself."

They continued to date and soon made it a twosome. Sure, he wandered off a couple of times when she put on a few pounds in the winter months, but he always came back to her for spring break. When he went off on his ski trips in January and February, and stayed in New Orleans for a couple of weeks around Mardi Gras, she was able to go to two packs a day, and get that weight lower for his return. She would never take any drug. Cigarettes were plenty for her.

When Mary was just 19 and Todd was 21, they married. Things went well for a while, but when they decided to have a child, she found it difficult to conceive. She was frantic from hearing Todd blame her, saying she must be doing something wrong. For a while she even went up to two and a half packs a day to deal with the stress.

She finally was able to get pregnant. Everything went fine, except the baby only weighed four and a half pounds at birth. She was well formed, but very tiny, and for the first month or two had a difficult time taking in enough formula. Mary was grossed out at the thought of breastfeeding and didn't want her top to be any bigger than it had been before. She quickly went from the pack a day during pregnancy back to two packs a day which, when added to her aerobic exercise, soon allowed her to return to her clothes from before pregnancy. Her periods did stop for a while, but she found a willing obstetrician who gave her a fertility drug when she wanted a second child. She certainly didn't want to be fat, even if that was the price for getting pregnant. She knew that modern science could take care of it. The second child, a boy, died shortly after birth, but the third one, also a boy, lived. She was sure that even though he was only five pounds at birth, he would eventually grow up to be big and tall like Todd.

Mary's lung cancer grew slowly. She had been getting mammograms and Pap smears since she was 30. It was only when she developed high cortisol levels from the ectopic, ACTH-secreting, small-cell carcinoma of the lung that she realized something might be wrong. She was no longer able to keep her weight or appetite under control. The many small blood vessels near the skin burst. The one consolation she had was her Maryland Thins. The one lung remaining after the surgery lasted for a while. When the doctor wasn't looking, she would take off her oxygen mask, turn to the side, open a window, and have another one of those wonderful, slimming friends.

No sir, no drugs for Mary—just good Maryland tobacco. Mary's two children eventually did well, although the girl had severe asthma until after her mother's death and the boy got so many ear infections that he eventually needed tubes. But all things considered, Mary had raised them as well as she could and was thankful she had never used any drugs. She did not want to set a bad example.

Comment

At the beginning of the 20th century, cigarettes were popularized for women with the advertisement that you should reach for a cigarette instead of a sweet. Television ads in the 60s and 70s purposely lured women into believing that cigarettes would keep them thin. Some studies have suggested that the probability of a teenage girl starting to smoke is directly proportional to the degree to which she values thinness and develops a morbid fear of fatness. Even in the use of illegal drugs, my experience is that a fair proportion, perhaps a third or so, of stimulant abuse in girls is not just for recreational purposes, but in the service of the eating disorder. A few drinks of alcohol are necessary help some anorexics to sleep, whereas coke or meth is sometimes used to pacify bulimic urges. In these cases, treatment for the eating disorder also addresses the drug use.

We overlook the fact that cigarettes are actually the most commonly used addictive drug. Yes, it's legal. But we certainly should prevent kids from getting hooked. Let's start by telling them to stay active and reach for a healthy treat or exercise instead of a ciggy. Better tasting. Better living. Better sex. Better breath. Better lungs. Better kids—without the smokes.

Originally published in 2002.

65

Sadism and Masochism: The Scale and the Mirror

weight obsession, body image, scales & mirrors

One day scale and mirror decided to wreak havoc on the earth. Scale decided that it would terrorize people from the moment they got up during the day 'til the moment they went to bed. Scale gradually infiltrated all the media until soon it became the thing to do to weigh yourself and to talk about how fat you were. Soon the nation was filled with people who felt bad when they weighed themselves in the morning. They approached the scale like a judge or God and pleaded that the number would be kind to them that day.

In the meantime Mirror decided it would create its own form of misery for the human race. Starting in the United States and Western Europe, Mirror would no longer be a small piece of glass in which a woman checked her lipstick and the hem of her dress and a man checked his tie. It soon became a leering, peering, distorted lens through which people could imagine themselves being unattractive, lumpy, and misproportioned.

"Hey Scale," said Mirror, "I'm going to get people to think that they're not perfect so they're horrible. Women will see themselves as having too big of a stomach, too large hips, fat thighs, and start believing there's nothing right about them except maybe their eyes or not even that. Men will look at themselves and think they are puny and skinny and unattractive, not at all like the men in the fitness magazines."

Soon, Scale and Mirror were wreaking their modern forms of sadism and masochism on the whole world. The use of large mirrors spread until people saw their reflections everywhere: in elevators, restrooms, along the walls of restaurants, and throughout their homes. Thus, people became more and more dissatisfied with themselves.

Along came Amazonia. She was captain of the Special Rescue Squad that The Counsel of Planets sent to Earth to save it from the sadistic practices of Scale and the masochistic practices of Mirror. Amazonia, with arms that could extend around the Earth and an ability to move at 99% of the speed of light, soon scooped up all the scales and threw them on a trajectory that would take them past Neptune and eventually out of the solar system. Amazonia clapped her titanium hands, and all the mirrors on the Earth cracked and bent, so that only small mirrors with wavy glass remained. At best, they could only be used to straighten one's hair or shave.

Very gradually, the misery and unhappiness of the human race receded. People got up in the morning, stretched their limbs, and went off to work, play, or school without first getting judged by a scale or suffering from the distorted message of the mirror coming through their cultural eyes. Amazonia went back to the Interplanetary Counsel but kept a close eye on Earth.

Comment:

As far as the happiness and comfort of human beings, the scale and the mirror have contributed very little. The scale has been given the power to judge people and make critical comments, telling them whether they will have a good day or a bad day, whether they are in fact good or bad people.

When you ask yourself why women who are 5'10" are not shortened and women who are 5'1" are not stretched on the rack, the answer is obvious: There's a normal natural variation in height. The same goes with weight but many people, and unfortunately too many doctors, think that a women or a man of a certain age and height should weigh exactly so many pounds. This is as ridiculous as saying that only women 5'5" should be considered normal. Much better are multiple predictors of fitness and health including waist-to-hip ratio, percent body fat, blood lipids (cholesterol, HDL, LDL, triglycerides), exercise capacity, and resting heart rate. If people would discard the scale and its pseudo-scientific BMI, they would be happier and healthier.

The same goes for the mirror. As mirrors have become larger and more prominent, people have become more and more unhappy. When you look into a mirror, you look into the eyes of cultural distortion. You also generally don't take a glance at the whole package and see how it hangs together, but rather start focusing on individual parts and deciding they're not perfect. This or that is too big. This or that is too small. This or that is out of proportion.

While scales inflict damage on others, the mirror lets an individual inflict damage on himself or herself—one definition of masochism. Why in the world would someone want to look in the mirror in the morning except to see that their tie is straight, their the hair is neat, and that there's no cream from the hot chocolate on their lips? The pseudo-objectivity of the mirror is an illusion. Looking in the mirror always leads to a distorted view of oneself.

Mirror gazing and asking the scale for affirmation of self are no-win situations that would better be abandoned since they're incapable of reform. Up with fitness, self-esteem, and mutual support. Down with the sadism of the scale, the masochism of the mirror.

Originally published in 2002.

66

Driving a RAC or a CAR?

bulimia, males, anger

Zach was totally amp'd on racecar driving. He even drove his everyday '74 Chevy "green whale" the same way he drove at the racetrack on weekends. The green whale was bigger than any car on the street. It was banged up a lot, and even scared the holy heck out of the taxi drivers in New York City. The 400 horses under the hood were only the start. The acceleration was fierce. The banged up body let people know they had to give way, not him. Of course, the dents and paint scrapes told a story. You looked at Zach the wrong way, and he moved into your lane in a microsecond and forced you to stop or go on the sidewalk. He even had a bumper sticker that said, "If you don't like my driving, stay off the sidewalk." Each dent was a notch on his belt that "taught those jerks a lesson."

With cobra-like speed, he expressed his anger at the slightest provocation. But why blame him? The taxi-drivers pissed him off with their attitudes. When his mother asked him not to smoke pot in the house, she pissed him off; he bolted out the door and took off. Stop lights that lasted too long only meant the city was going to the dogs. When he thought they had been red long enough, he lit out. The stupid guy he thought was a buddy suggested the half-dozen six-packs he had each week were going to his belly. He'd show his old friend. After dinner, or a bunch of beers, he started to make himself vomit. He'd get a real "six-pack." Of course, his girlfriend knew better than to contradict him. She just happened to have a couple of black eyes from hitting "doorknobs," or at least that was what she told the emergency room staff. After all, she also annoyed him when she made any suggestions about his behavior.

After a long time of trying every approach, his mom, his racing coach, and his traitor buddy did an intervention and told him it was either treatment in hospital or jail. He chose hospital, but boy, was he ever pissed off, and told that to every staff member. In the men's eating disorders group, he gave every reason why the world was filled with idiots, his mother was out of date, and he had a right to express his anger. In fact, why were they bugging him about his feelings? After all, psychiatry says you should express your feelings.

Bud, his social worker and co-leader of the group, gradually got his attention. "Hey, Zach, why drive a RAC when you could drive a CAR?"

"What are you frigging talking about, you nerd? Can't you spell?" Zach asked. Bud took a moment to think, and then said, "Well, Zach, a RAC, like the RAC you've been driving, is really short-hand for Reactive Anger Condition. What I'm suggesting is that you switch to driving a CAR, a Chosen Anger Response. The deal is, learn to respond, not react. You're no better right now than a mad dog that responds to every breeze or noise. Sometime, I hope soon, you'll learn the only thing you can control in life is yourself. Sure, anger is okay; it's a perfectly normal feeling. But it's not okay to react with any old behavior when you have an angry feeling. You're clueless now about when you are angry. Get it up on your radar screen. Give it a name. Then figure out how to respond with a chosen behavior that's good for you and those around you. Your empathy quotient sucks, Zach, by the way."

Zach thought this was hogwash (actually he used another term). But, a bit at a time, he started learning to identify anger as anger, as an okay feeling, and then to wait a while, and decide on what behavior he wanted to choose. It made him feel surprisingly good to choose. After, all, it was like choosing a gear on the car in a race. You didn't just throw the clutch into any gear, but chose the one that fitted the situation on the racetrack. Corners were different from straightaways. He still got pissed off easily, but stopped the binge-purge, told his mother she wasn't so bad, and his girlfriend, mysteriously, stopped getting shiners from hitting high door knobs. Zach was off to the race, the real race—life. And make that a marathon, not a sprint, Zach.

Comment

How many therapists haven't been faced with young people with eating disorders who fuel their eating disorders, as well as their aggressive behavior, by highly intense, inappropriate anger that they don't realize is a problem. A good question to ask eating disordered young guys with reactive anger, is, "What's your piece in all of this—when you purge, when you scare the heck out of other drivers, when you hit your girlfriend? What's your piece?"

Most of the time, this is a therapeutic learning challenge—to teach a hot reactor to slow down his reactivity to the anger, to respond, not to react. Change that instant reactivity to a chosen response. And, by the way, you'll pick up a bit of empathy in loose change along the way. Life will definitely be less confusing to guys like Zach struggling with anger and eating disorders. With therapy, and sometimes medication as a partner, get your patients to trade in the RAC for a CAR. Life drives a lot better that way.

Originally published in 2003.

67

The Parakeet Pancake

control, perfectionism, recovery tool

Polly very much wanted a parakeet. After showing her parents that she could do her homework and clean her room, they gave her the money to buy a parakeet. Polly brought it home and named it Patty. Polly reached into the cage to get Patty familiar with her and to practice letting it perch comfortably on her hand. But, of course, she did not want it to fly away and become a snack for the cat or fly out the door. So after Polly reached in, she held Patty very tightly, bringing it out with both hands around the bird. She would not let this parakeet fly away and get into trouble. No way. Soon, there was no more parakeet, at least no more squirming, squawking, wriggling parakeet. There was only parakeet pancake. Oops. Too tight.

Of course, Polly was devastated. Her parents understood that she had no experience with birds before and volunteered to buy her a new parakeet. This time Polly knew she did not want to hold the parakeet so tightly that it became a pancake. So she reached in very gently and brought Penny out, holding her very loosely in her cupped hands. The parakeet soon flew out into the room. On one of its swooping flights down to the lower part of the room, Penny barely missed the cat's claws as it leapt up. The parakeet flew around and around. Penny soon found an open window and away she went into the unknown. Oops. Too loose.

Polly was embarrassed to tell her parents about the second parakeet. In fact, she didn't say anything. She took the money she had earned from babysitting and allowance and went down to the pet store to buy a third parakeet (Peggy) that looked as much like the second one as possible.

Polly reached into the cage after Peggy had adjusted to the new cage and brought it out with two hands. She held the parakeet just tightly enough so it didn't escape into the room where the dangerous cat could snatch it or where it could fly away. She kept it loose enough so she could lightly feel its heartbeat and fluttering wings. She felt the parakeet relax. Soon, she calmed the parakeet and gave it little bits of lettuce and sunflower seeds while holding it with the right amount of gentle control in her cupped hands. Gradually, the parakeet learned that it was safe in her cupped hands. It learned it could walk out on Polly's finger and then back into her hands because the parakeet knew that Polly cared for it and it was safe. Not too tight, not too loose, safety and freedom.

Comment

Over-control often leads to out of control. Many anorexia nervosa patients show perfectionistic features trying to control events, relationships, schoolwork, hobbies and feelings far beyond what is possible. Too tightly controlling any of these main areas of adolescent challenge usually leads to the next response of getting out of control: going from a perfect room to a sloppy room, from anorexic tendencies to out of control binge behavior, from over-compliance to defiance.

Although it may feel threatening at first, patients benefit from learning how to achieve moderate, reasonable control for life's challenges, not using excessive unnecessary energy to achieve impossible levels of control. If you gently teach them about the parakeet pancake versus the parakeet that ran away, they often get the idea. Although most eating disorder programs do not follow the 12-step principles, there is one strong parallel applicable to young eating disordered patients—learning what things can be controlled, what things can not be controlled, and gaining the wisdom to know the difference. Adequate control rather then "perfect" control is critical to success. Perfection is actually the enemy not their friend. Perfectionism is a monster than can never be satisfied.

How much is reasonable control? That's something that can be worked out situation by situation, person by person, but it's usually not that hard compared to the impossibility of excessive perfectionistic control or facing the consequences of no control. Remember Polly and the parakeet pancake.

Originally published in 2003.

68

Taking the Train from Station A to B

anorexia nervosa, cognitive distortion, magical thinking, anxiety

Allie went to the train station to get a ticket from A, where she started, to B, where she wanted to go. She had looked on the map and saw that the train went from A to B to C. As she looked up on the schedule for the train, she saw that the train left A at 1 p.m., arrived at B at 2 p.m., and then at C at 3 p.m.

For some unjustifiable reason, Allie was extremely afraid that the train would go directly from A to C, which was definitely a place she did not want to go. She absolutely, under no condition, wanted to go to C. The map said the train went from A to B to C. The schedule said the train went from A to B to C. But Allie was skeptical and thought it might skip over B or speed past without stopping.

So Allie stepped back and saw what other people did. A friend of hers, Sandy, said hi to Allie and then bought a ticket from A to B. Allie asked Sandy if she would call Allie on her cell phone when Sandy got to B. Sandy said, "Sure, I will."

A little more than an hour later, Sandy called Allie on her cell phone and said, "Hi Allie. This is Sandy. I got off at B, just as planned."

Another friend of Allie's, Jack, came along and after saying hi to Allie, bought a ticket from A to B. He also called when he got to B and said it was a fine ride, and the train stopped at B, where he departed. Allie still didn't trust that the train would stop at B. Poor Allie. She was so afraid the train would change its schedule and somehow magically skip B, so she never got on the train.

Comment

So many anorexia nervosa patients are sure that as soon as they stop being starved they will be fat. It's almost as if the moment they are no longer starved they fall over a cliff and hurdle into obesity valley. I use the story of the train with many of them. The challenge is getting the patient to truly believe that trains that have a track going from A to B to C always have to go through B before going on C. This applies in the transition from starved to healthy to overweight. Somehow they're sure the train will jump over B and go right to C.

Although no analogies are perfect and none of them can take the place of the hard work of Cognitive Behavioral Therapy and interpersonal therapy, they may help patients to challenge the belief that physics and trains don't work for them like they do for all other people. We try to help them reframe the unhealthy visual image with ones that allow them to truly believe that getting better from starvation means stopping at B, not hurtling on to C. This story may counteract the idea that they go from starvation to fatness. Getting them to accept that they can get off the train at B without going to C is a potentially important first step in challenging all or none reasoning—the anticipatory anxiety and avoiding of attaining normal weight.

Originally published in 2003.

69

Radio Station FATT

weight loss, weight prejudice

This is radio station FATT coming to you 24 hours a day, 7 days a week on a very strong transmitter. Keep that radio station tuned in to FATT, 0099 on your dial!

Here's our program for the week. First, we will have several accounts on how America is getting fat. Next, we will tell you seven new ways of losing weight rapidly, five pounds a week guaranteed. We will interview several people who have finally found happiness through self-starvation. The high point of today's program will be six new ways to flush fat from your body, ten proven techniques to bring up your lunch in the restroom, and a new treadmill that will make you work harder than any machine you've ever tried.

Radio station FATT is dedicated to your happiness, your sense of control, your ability to be perfect. Hear our strategies so you'll never be teased or criticized, new ways to control family disagreements, ways to finally come out of the shadow of your sister's outgoing personality, ways to give you the recognition that you never got as one of those disgustingly average "normal" people.

FATT is proud to announce that in addition to broadcasting to every country in North and South America and all of Europe, it is expanding rapidly into 24-hour service to remote islands in the Pacific and the Northern most provinces of China, Russia, and Korea. Next year, we will cover the globe completely and will be able to beam our stations to any spaceships that are launched. We have become partners in the pro-anorexia web sites that are now popping up whenever some innocent dupe asks for information about diet, health, weight, food, or beauty. Radio station FATT has become standard in 93% of elevators and in 79% of telephones in place of a busy signal. We aim for 100%.

We offer special rates to advertisers, especially to those who offer weight loss programs, over-the-counter weight loss drugs, and new "natural products" for cleansing. We promote offers for high-intensity exercise machines, ads for spas that specialize in rapid weight loss, and ultra-low calorie life-styles, including the new "ribs are beautiful" programs. We are proposing that there be dispensers of Ipecac in every college dorm and at the end of cafeteria lines.

Comment

While there's no single radio station with the call letters "FATT," the sum total of all the broadcast craziness on radio and television stations promoting weight loss is equivalent to a worldwide station broadcasting unhealthy weight and behavior around the clock. As with many of those tunes you can't get out of your head, so many of these advertisements and "programs" on FATT stick in your mind despite the common myth that that products don't do much and should never be taken seriously. Why would advertisers spend money on these ads if there were no pay-off? When these ads relentlessly promote weight loss, they become internalized, worsening body image even for well adjusted people, and they drive the eating disordered individuals harder and harder until almost no one questions these ads. Eventually, the listeners can't distinguish between the propaganda from FATT and what is true and healthy. There is nothing as effective as a truly big lie repeated over and over again.

STORIES I TELL MY PATIENTS

Suggesting to patients that they in fact have been tuning in to radio station FATT helps them recognize the brain washing and propaganda that's going on all around them and can help them to becoming critical of inappropriate media. Using the idea of a radio receiver being necessary to hear the contents of FATT, the patients learn that they can turn the volume down, switch to another station, or pull the plug on the radio. All are techniques that grow logically out of the mental image of an eating disordered patient being a receiver for radio station FATT.

Originally published in 2003.

70

It's All Greek to Me

all ED, assertiveness, laxatives, exercise

Reggie was eating her 11 Cheerios slowly. She had managed to eat three when her mother reminded her she hadn't done her Spanish homework. Reggie complied, but first she dumped her remaining eight Cheerios on the floor, where the dog quickly gobbled them. At the same time, Brittany, in her home, was having breakfast when her dad scolded her for her messy room. She scurried up to the bedroom, fixed up the room, and took off to school in her used VW. But before she hit the first class, she had eaten a dozen donuts. Meanwhile, Pam was mulling over in her mind the argument she had had with her boyfriend. After a healthy breakfast of cereal, fruit, and milk in front of her parents, she took a quick shower, worrying that the breakfast she purged in the shower would clog the plumbing like it did last week.

Across town, Lucy skipped her breakfast, as usual. Today, her ballet teacher would tell her whether or not she made the front line. That extra dozen laxatives would work before the late afternoon dance class, and that was sure to help. The fifth of the quintet of pals, Elaine, her parents' argument still ringing in her head from last night, glanced at her watch and realized she could get in another half hour on the exercise bike before going to school. That would make her feel better. Of course, the hour of pushups and sit-ups in the middle of the night left her a bit tired, but Coach would be happy when she told him about her extra exercise.

What a day it was in school! The Spanish test was harder than Reggie had thought it would be. She decided to skip her no-fat yogurt for lunch. Mom and Dad would understand that she couldn't make it to supper, as usual. During the study periods, Brittany gazed at the teen magazine that she had tucked into her backpack. Then she looked with envy at her friend Mimi, who was so long and thin. What a ball of fat she was by comparison with Mimi. No lunch today! But later, she couldn't avoid ordering the super-special at McDonald's later, and then on to the Burger King deluxe burger and fries. Why bother trying to avoid the extra-large Blizzard at the DQ? At least she would feel better. Some other day, she would work on looking like Mimi.

Lucy was really scared of being told by her ballet teacher she had gained weight, so she took another handful of laxatives before dance class. Scary, scary, scary to face her teacher, a real Russian-trained autocrat. Now, she would be sure her belly didn't stick out. Of course, she worried she might faint, but she would just have to accept the risk. At the same time, the cross country coach was pushing Elaine to run faster and faster, and reminded her not to have any candy, fats, or fast-burning carbs. She was already down to 94 pounds at five feet three inches, but knew that a little more exercise would make Coach smile, so she went all out. She figured not having periods for six months wasn't all that unusual for a 10th grader.

And so it went, day after day. Reggie restricted whenever life was tough, but she didn't have such bad feelings as long as she watched the calories and fat grams. Brittany felt crummy much of the time, but the quick-fix binges took care of that, at least for a couple of hours. Pam was known to disappear soon after she had a snack with her friends, especially when she had talked about how her boyfriend's anger. For the first time she could remember, Elaine felt good about herself and forgot about the fights at home; and, Lucy had the solution to pleasing the Russian ballet coach right in her purse.

One night, each of these girls had dreams that puzzled her when she woke up the next morning. In her dream, Reggie had stopped counting out her Cheerios and took a full bowl. When her mother reminded her about her Spanish homework, she said, "You know, Mom, when you remind me for the fifth time about the Spanish homework, I feel anxious. I would like it if you could remind me once, and then let me take care of it. I'm old enough to make my own decisions about homework." In Brittany's dream, she said, "Dad, I get angry feelings when you scold me about having a messy room. It's my room, and I'll take care of it on Saturday. Would you please hold off the reprimand." She also saw herself on the cover of the next issue of *Glamour*, being featured for her normality, with Mimi looking enviously at her.

Elaine dreamed that she was ten feet tall. In the dream, when Dad yelled at Mom, she told him, "Why don't you just settle down and talk instead of getting so upset?" Another vision came to Elaine in her dream. In it, she was a perfectly healthy weight, with lots of flexibility and muscle tone. She told her coach to take a long walk on a short pier, "It makes me furious when you push me and the other girls to run faster and faster even when our knees hurt. And it's completely unnecessary to cut out fun foods in moderation. We don't need your approval to feel good about ourselves. I would like you to find a new career, preferably as a prison guard or a janitor." And then she ran a mile in three minutes and forty-five seconds!

Lucy's dream was like a Chagall painting. In it, she dreamed she danced like Margot Fontaine, the glamorous ballerina of past years. She flew up into the air on her angel-wings, doing 20 consecutive complete turns, as she flew with perfect form from housetop to housetop, finally dumping a bucket of coal dust on her tyrannical teacher. She then humbly turned to the audience for a standing ovation. As she left the stage, she said, "Oh Russian dance teacher, your demands make me furious and then depressed. I wish you would give us some encouragement once in a while. That would make me happy."

Lastly, Pam saw herself telling her boyfriend, "It makes me sad and angry when you care for me one day and criticize me the next. I don't need a guy to feel good about myself. I would really like it if you would make up your mind and be consistent. In the meantime, grow up. And the answer is "No" to that weekend at your house when your parents are away." Then, she walked away calmly and confidently.

These dreams were puzzling until the five girls met in their eating disorders group therapy that evening. Their counselor said, "You know, eating disorders are a language. As long as emotions are Greek to you, so to speak, the eating disorder behavior is the only language you really speak. So let's spend this session giving names to feelings and learning the *assertive triad*."

Comment

Eating disorders are really a language for expressing unpleasant emotions—like fear of growing up, sadness, envy, and anger. But as long as these feelings stay out of conscious recognition, with no names for them, it's all "Greek," a foreign tongue, a form of alexithymia to the patient. They have learned to indirectly express their emotions through eating disordered behaviors, even though these behaviors are unhealthy.

Patients with eating disorders benefit from learning to accurately identify and express their feelings, as in using the *assertive triad*. Here's how it works. Fill in the three blanks: "When you _____ (the other person's behavior that is making you upset), I feel _____ (your emotion). I would like you to _____ (how you would like the other person to behave.). Example, "When you fight in front of me, Mom and Dad, I feel helpless but angry. I would like you guys to get some marriage therapy to help you communicate without fighting."

This triad also works for good feelings. "When you give me a genuine compliment, it makes me feel good, even though it's hard for me to accept it's true. Please keep it up, especially to reinforce my taking care of myself in healthy ways."

Greek is a fine language that originated nearly five millenia ago. It's wonderful to learn Greek, especially for academic scholars. But let's not express our emotions in an ancient language, when we can speak more clearly in our native tongue.

Originally published in 2003.

71

A Speck of Dust

anorexia nervosa, control, quality of life

If only I could become a speck of dust. If I could lose more weight, become smaller and smaller, eventually I would like to be like that speck of dust in the corner of the ceiling. Then, my friends wouldn't tease me and say I have big hips and thunder thighs. I could watch them tease someone else. I'd be so tiny that my parents wouldn't bug me about everything, and my baby sister wouldn't be so clingy. They wouldn't even see me.

If I were a speck of dust, I would have been safe from that guy who was drunk at my best friend's party. Maybe I wouldn't regret our lost friendship if she didn't say I was asking for it. If no one could see me, I wouldn't have to deal with everyone's questions about it all. It would be so much safer to be a speck of dust, a molecule floating in space. Then, I could see all the people being sorry for me and regretting how badly they treated me, but no one could see me.

I'm not there yet, but I'm losing more and more weight. I've lost most of that ugly fat, and soon I'll be able to wear children's jeans. I can hide in the shadow of a slim tree! I'm getting smaller and smaller, safer and safer. Maybe in a few more weeks I'll be there. They'll all wonder where I've gone, but I'll be able to see them.

Comment

Although patients with anorexia nervosa intellectually understand that they'll never shrink away to a speck of dust, they often have the magical idea that safety lies in becoming smaller and smaller—fading into the woodwork. The fantasy is that from the position of a speck they can see without being observed, they can watch others but be free from criticism and hurt. The emotional logic is very clear. While there are probably many dynamics behind anorexia nervosa, certainly one of them is to literally become so small that there is safety through invisibility—protection through inaccessibility.

An important part of treatment is helping patients recognize that their need for personal safety is completely normal and understandable, but thinness is not protective. We need to help these patients learn that the bad situations they have experienced can be worked through, and they can develop skills and confidence to more securely meet new challenges. Their fears often reflect the anticipatory anxiety of their vulnerable personality or dread that the past will be repeated.

The goal is to recognize that most of life's situations can be handled skillfully as they progress in learning direct ways to deal with problems, emotions, and relationships. Being a speck of dust really isn't much fun. It gets lonely to not be hugged. You couldn't experience joy and contentment, satisfaction and meaning, love or growth. It really isn't effective to become a speck of dust; better to be assertive and be a substantial person

Originally published in 2003.

72

Life's Black Hole

self-harm, emotional intensity disorder, depression

Ellen was struggling. She spun around and around getting closer to the black hole. She knew that once she entered the vacancy of the black hole, it was all over. No one could understand what she was going through. She couldn't explain the feeling of never-ending emptiness, of her aloneness. This must be what Hell is like. In the pocket of her jeans, she had a small knife. She drew it out and cut two shallow lines on her wrist. There it was—the magical red color, and as she looked at it, she gathered her strength, grabbed hold of the nearest light beam, and slowly crawled out of the grip of the black hole's vortex. Escape, for a day at least.

When she returned to galactic school that day, she made sure she wore her long titanium-based turtleneck that ended just below the crease of the wrist. Back to the lessons on quantum travel agency rules. Nobody would notice her cuts.

The teacher, Kristaxi from alpha-centuri was just fantastic—what a dish— with his curly mop of hair and deep voice, along with the extra arms so he could draw in four colors at once to illustrate a point. She loved his class and secretly loved him. She even dreamed of a long honeymoon together on the glowing beaches of Beta-3. Kristaxi called on

Ellen and asked her to summarize the homework from last night—the section on minimizing time travel between inter-galactic stations. Ellen panicked— she had forgotten all about it. What a rat he was to call on her. He should have known she had a difficult night. Instead of taking responsibility for not doing her homework, she was angry that he called on her. Marry that guy, what was she thinking? She hated him and rudely said, "Well, I heard you have never actually traveled to even the closest galaxy, so how can you teach us about it?"

Now, she felt bad. She had gone back to the old pattern of love turning to hate, admiration to demeaning. As soon as a break came, she went into the fluids room to relieve herself. The bad feeling was getting worse—it was turning into the Void. Closing herself in one of the stalls she drew out her trusty knife. This time, the left arm—the old scars had almost healed there. The black hole was pulling her; the emptiness descended on her. She felt herself spinning into the vortex of nameless horror that no one else understood. She couldn't even give it a name. She would scream, if it would do any good.

Instead, she slowly made a cut from elbow to wrist, a little deeper this time. For the first time, she could see a vein with dark blood, and just below, a pulsing red artery. As the blood trickled down her arm into the fluid-disposal shaft, she felt the beginning of relief. The black hole let go of its grip.

Comment

Paradoxically, when people harm themselves, they escape the pain from their terrifying feelings. Instead of confronting their emotions, they feel like a black hole is sucking them into a vortex of crushing intensity. These patients need empathy and compassion, as well as limits. By naming the feelings (anxiety, fear, sadness, guilt), they can recognize that the emotions don't need to be boundless and all encompassing. With professional help, these individuals can wait out the experience, realize the black hole is in their mind, and make more skillful choices that truly help, and don't only provide temporary diversions from their distress. They may cling to their cycles of emotional intensity, impulsivity, self-harm, and abandonment fears but, they need care, not abandonment or false rescues.

Originally published in 2003.

73

Terrors in the Forest

perfectionism, quality of life, anorexia nervosa

Becky liked horror flicks as much as any kid, but this was no movie—this was real. She was in a forest, and a monster was stalking her. She heard its steps—thud, thud, thud—relentlessly coming after her. She saw its lime green color. She felt its hot breath, and sensed its long, snake-like tongue trying to find her. The monster was horrifying and it caught her! She struggled and struggled, and suddenly broke free from its grip. But then it came after her again, trying to seize her.

As she backed away, she realized she had stepped into quicksand. She felt herself sinking slowly, being sucked deeper and deeper. Then she remembered, if she stopped flailing and tried floating, like in the sea, she might make it. She did, but barely.

Still shaking from the quicksand, she could only relax for a moment, because then the monster came after her again. Doubting she could free herself again, she fought, and was about to give up, but then she thought to completely relax. She felt the monster let go of its grip for a brief moment—just long enough for her to escape.

She had to get away. She ran furiously through the forest. Oh, no! Another pool of quicksand. What an experience! No more movies ever, if

I get out of this living nightmare. I know what real monsters and quicksand are like. They suck.

But unlike movies, this experience did not stop. The monster, then the quicksand. Then the monster, then the quicksand. Over and over. They never stopped.

Comment

Perfectionism is a monster. Comparisons with others is quicksand. Not *like* a monster. Not *like* quicksand. Perfectionism *is* a monster. Comparing yourself to others *is* quicksand. Both are terrorizing. They are everyday, never-ending, nightmare-like, real life terrors. Just when you get out of the grip of one, the other gets you. There is no relief. No rest. No peace. Life is an alternation between one and the other.

Perfectionism seems attractive to many patients suffering from anorexia nervosa. They often say things like, "I have to do things perfectly. I think that all the time. I feel it inside. But I can't ever do things perfectly—except I can be a perfect anorexic. And no one is going to take that away from me. Anorexia is the only thing I am really good at."

The healthy alternative is totally achievable, reality-based, satisfying and effective. It means being fully adequate and competent, "plenty good enough." Try asking patients to complete the sentence, "Anything worth doing is worth doing _____ (what)." The usual answer is "well." If the patient is a perfectionist, I suggest instead that they try out the phrase, "Anything worth doing is worth doing badly." If they will simply start something they had previously demanded that they do perfectly, instead planning to do things "badly," surprise, surprise, they will usually do it plenty good enough.

Comparison with others is quicksand—especially the kind of comparisons our anorexia nervosa patients practice. When is the last time one of these patients practiced "objective" comparison. It's always. "Jane is thinner. Francine is more attractive. Zoe is smarter." The others are always better in some way. We help patients get out of the comparison trap and find value from their own selves.

Help patients out of the forest with the monster of perfectionism and the pools of quicksand onto safe ground with adequate competence and an inner compass.

Originally published in 2004.

74

The Rat Race

quality of life, anxiety

Athletes do it. Lawyers do it. Scientists do it. Dieters do it. Pals do it. Neighbors do it. The Rat Race! Ready, get set, go! Line up. Look left and right. Get off that mark faster. Compete harder. Keep it up. Stay in the lead. If they get something, you go for more. Show them. Don't let them get ahead. Move your butt. Stop making excuses. Pour on the steam. No whining. Keep it up.

Oh, by the way, at the end of the rat race, you're still a rat. There is no finish line, no prize, no winners. Only rats keep racing with no end in sight. But, what the heck, keep going. Or, maybe not.

Comment

Juliet Schorr, Ph.D., Professor of Sociology at Boston College, internationally recognized economist, researcher, and former Director of Women's Studies Program at Harvard University, authored the devastatingly accurate books, *The Overworked American: The Unexpected Decline of Leisure,* and *The Overspent American: Upscaling, Downshifting, and the New Consumer.* In a lecture I heard her give, she used the analogy of a football game. There's an exciting play on the field. The first row stands up, the second row stands up, then the third row, and so forth. Soon, no one can see better than when they were all sitting down.

One of the biggest falsehoods from the 1970s was the confident prediction that in 20 years working people in the U.S. would be working less than 30 hours a week and would need help managing their leisure time. However, instead of having too much leisure time, people now are working more and more, trying to get a little bit ahead, making what used to be luxuries into necessities. Sure, some folks absolutely need to work their heads off trying to make ends meet. But there are many other folks who have traded leisure time for more time at the office. They have stopped participating in community activities, rarely see or talk to their neighbors, and communicate urgency and stress to their kids that they need to get ahead of their friends—their competitors.

As a result, quality of life has seriously suffered. The rat race is in full swing. Absolutely, everyone needs a decent wage and enough for life's necessities; but, most people do not need lots of the things they are competing for and stressing about. Especially, they don't need to get thinner than others in the race for weight loss. Stop the rat race. Get a life. Chill. Enjoy. Get a life of balance and meaning.

Originally published in 2004.

75

Fire Those Servants

recovery tool, all ED, weight prejudice

Queen Betty ruled over her kingdom with great skill and was much loved. She lived in Buckinglamb Palace with many servants. One day, a servant named Armeenie looked at the Queen and said to her, "My, you are getting fat." Queen Betty didn't know what to say, but decided to overlook this insult because of the servant's past loyalty. A second servant, DeeOr spoke to the Queen as she passed from one room to another, saying, "You have big hips, Queen Betty." Never before had a servant said such an outrageous thing to her. She was thinking about what to do when a third servant, Versoochee, mumbled as he passed by, saying, "You are getting big, big, big."

Queen Betty went to the mirror and took a close look at herself. She was her usual vibrant, smart, fit self. Of course, horseback riding, hiking in the mountains, and jogging with the dogs all change a person's body size and shape slightly, as do lots of other normal activities. As she looked again in the mirror with her true eyes, she affirmed that she was a terrific person and decided it was silly to ask a dumb piece of mirrored glass whether she should like herself. That's it for mirrors except checking whether her crown was on the right way.

FIRE THOSE SERVANTS

Queen Betty knew what she was going to do. Her mind was made up. "Fire those lousy, disloyal servants that give stupid, negative, inappropriate messages. They work for me. I don't work for them." She turned on her heel and approached Armeenie with dignity. "Armeenie, you are fired. How dare you be so rude. Leave right now." Next, she found DeeOr and spoke to her severely, "DeeOr, your employment is terminated immediately." Lastly, she located Versoochee and issued these clipped words: "I don't know what has happened to you, but you have crossed the line. In the olden days, it would have been off with your head, but we haven't practiced that sentence for a while. Out! Out! Out!"

The Queen looked over a list of applicants to replace the fired servants. She identified a number who had good recommendations and interviewed them personally. The servants she hired were pleasant, thoughtful, loyal, and smart looking. They worked out fine over the next several years, but in the back of her mind she knew that if these servants became rude, she would fire them right away.

Comment

Clothes are servants, not rulers or critics. When servants are rude and make critical remarks, for example, saying to a person that they are fat, hippy, big, ugly, and so on, those clothes need to be fired by taking them to a thrift store or thrown away. Don't hold on thinking you might go back to that size or style; for goodness sake, get rid of them. When there is a misfit between clothes and a person (the clothes are too tight, too short, etc.), why does the person assume that the clothes are right and that they are wrong. No! No! Fire the clothes.

Wear clothes that work for you. Don't work for the clothes. Hire them, fire them, change them, rule them thoughtfully. You are the ruler. They are the servants.

Originally published in 2004.

76

The Retirement Dinner

transition to puberty, anorexia nervosa, anxiety

Thank you for coming to this very important event in my life. Others sometimes face this event with peace, but for me, it is very stressful. I don't have a choice; it is something that I have to go through.

As I look back on the high points of my life, I remember especially those times when I was in "the zone" and everything seemed to work together and go right. During these high points, all the hard preparation that I had gone through earlier in life was paying off. It was wonderful to bring together my hard-earned knowledge, skills, and experience. I had that wonderful sense of control, of being on top of things. Life was good.

This time of change that I am going through is a time of crisis. Some-one told me once that in both Greek and Chinese, the word crisis means a time of danger as well as a time of opportunity. But I can only see the danger. Perhaps others can see the opportunity when they have had to face a similar situation, but that is not true for me.

It is truly frightening to age, to face an uncertain future now that the meaningful and productive time of life is over. My body is changing. My mind is changing. People are changing in the way they treat me. I just don't know what to do or how to act. It is not just frightening to grow old, it is embarrassing and risky.

My body, as it ages, is terrifying look at in the mirror. It is terrifying to live inside of it. Nothing is the way it used to be during those stable, golden, productive years that are past. The things that are happening to my body have never happened to me before. My mind works differently, too. I can't think as logically as I used to think. Maybe scientists will eventually find a way to stop this process of change, but they haven't found it yet.

I feel so helpless. Everything is so overwhelming. No one really prepared me for this. Sure, there were hints years ago about what was going to happen to me eventually. People even said transition could not be avoided. But I never knew it would be this bad. At least I can live on the rich dreams of my past happiness, but I am already having nightmares about the life that starts tomorrow.

Pray for me. Pray that I will not be completely helpless in the raging currents of the river I am crossing. I have no life jacket, boat, or oars. It is impossible to believe I can safely cross over to a future that can only go downhill, but maybe I will still have a few moments of happiness now and then, if only I can forget for a while what is happening to me.

But I don't want to end on a pessimistic note. I will never forget that you took the time to support me as the golden years become only faint memories. Thank you for the watch you gave me to keep track of the relentlessness of time. Thank you from the bottom of my heart for coming to my 13th birthday.

Comment

The transition to puberty can be incredibly terrifying to girls who have had a golden time in late childhood, in that pre-adolescent, pre-pubertal phase, when things seem to be working so well and life seems pretty predictable. Smart, perfectionistic, sensitive girls who have successfully worked though the central challenge of the pre-pubertal stage often have a sense of control and effectiveness. During this time, they may get all A's in school, are praised for their abilities, appearance, behavior, and for being a model child.

And then all hell breaks loose. They didn't ask for breasts and curves. Suddenly guys are noticing them for all the wrong reasons. The first menstrual cycle is freaky. Why am I bleeding? Something terrible must be wrong with me. I can't think logically. My moods are all over the place. School work is no longer a set of exercises that have obvious right answers. Being challenged to understand and analyze ambiguous poetry or stories with no right or wrong answers is confusing. The previous approach so successful pre-pubertally—of working harder, getting all the details right, handing in assignments with perfect answers and penmanship—doesn't necessarily work anymore.

Some of these girls were really happy tomboys (without gender conflict). They climbed trees, threw a ball, had guys as pals. Everyone patted them on the head for doing everything so well. Arthur Crisp, in his book, *Anorexia Nervosa: Let Me Be,* describes the use of anorexia nervosa as a defense against the existential fears of maturation. Some perfectionistic, sensitive girls who are confused and terrified by the pubertal changes that they did not ask for and do not understand will do anything to turn back the clock to that period of safety and control, the golden pre-pubertal years.

Clinicians treating these girls have a major task of helping them negotiate the pubertal process, of accepting, understanding, embracing, and working with and within these changes in body, mind, mood, and social interaction. If a young girl retreats to the pre-pubertal stage because of fears of maturation by developing anorexia nervosa, she can not go on to successfully meet and resolve the central challenge of adolescence: working out a secure personal identity. Adolescence is messy, a time of trial and error. "This isn't the daughter I know. She never acted this way before?" How often have I heard this lament!

Often, early teen girls can't make sense of the way their moods change. They may not be prepared for the different ways guys see them and treat them. Old friends become distant. They may want to roll back the time machine,—retreat to the safety of the pre-pubertal years when everything seemed under control. Anorexia nervosa is the seemingly perfect defense against maturational fears. But it only works in an illusory way by binding the maturational fears with cords of gold-plated steel that create a prison. In the end, anorexia nervosa is a disaster, creating the illusion of safety and control, while it steadily robs the young girl of a chance at growth and happiness.

With support, skill building, empowerment, assertiveness, and guidance in developing a confident body image, the early adolescent girl can have a very positive experience through these years. The future need not be, for these girls, nearly as scary as it seems when they understand what is happening and the reasons for the changes in mood and thinking. As they develop confidence in new social skills, discover the joys of having the body of a young woman, and develop meaningful relationships, adolescence becomes a positive experience. Let's help them see it as a bridge they can walk over step by step, not a fearful river of rapids and risky currents tossing them about with no boat or oars.

Originally published in 2004.

77

Inside the Eggerson's House

family dynamics, males, anorexia nervosa, exercise

The outside of the Eggerson house looked normal—sort of a 1950s split level in a development with similar houses. But inside, that's another story. Eggie was a 17-year-old guy who wanted to become the state champ of the 132 pound weight class. Since the third grade, he had gone out for wrestling, plus wrestling camp each summer, and last year to the University of Iowa Summer Wrestling Program, where the champion wrestler of all time, Dan Gable, had coached the Iowa team to 15 national wins.

The problem was that Eggie was 5'10" tall, and had hit 160 pounds when he was 15. No way he would put up with that. He ate only proteins, ran for at least an hour each day, hit the weight machines for two hours a day, and worked out in a tight rubber sweat suit even though it was against regulations. Finally he got down to 135 pounds, and by drinking no water for 24 hours before the weigh in, he just made it at 131.5 pounds.

Eggie had become irritable, isolated, talking about nothing else but getting his weight down. Of course, no one knew he made himself throw up after family meals, when he ate what his parents fixed for supper. They picked up the hint from Eggie that carbohydrates were repulsive to him, and that he might do something drastic if they didn't go along with his exercise and weight loss plan. "Please, Eggie, try this casserole." The ferocious look they got told them to back off. They shopped for the leanest ostrich meat, but Eggie said it was still too fat. So they tried to find chicken raised organically. Finally, he said, "Vegetables and nuts, that's all."

Mom and Dad walked on eggshells so he wouldn't be upset with them. When Mom suggested a visit to an eating disorders clinic, he left the house and ran for two hours, coming back so ragged looking they were really afraid. "See what you made me do," Eggie said. When they found his diary they opened it—big mistake. He listed every calorie he had eaten, how many times he had to stick his finger down his throat to make himself sick, and how fat he was when he looked in the mirror. He'd written phrases such as, "Can't go on with life if I get fat . . . pile of blubber, that's me . . . coach will send me packing if I go above this weight."

When Dad suggested a movie, he said he didn't have time, "Stop pestering me. If you hadn't give me these genetics, my life would be fine." Mom wondered what she had done wrong. Of course, they couldn't talk to their friends, because Eggie would be furious. When Dad tried to give him a hug, he felt how cold Eggie's skin was and noticed how blue Eggie's fingers had become.

They went with a double layer of eggshells on their shoes to see his wrestling match. When he fell backwards and fainted in the first period, the ref called the match, and the team doc hurried up to examine Eggie. His heart rate was only 32 beats a minute. His blood pressure, even when he came to, was 85/45, and his hematocrit was 59, way above normal—from taking powerful diuretics and dehydrating himself. Eggie didn't have a choice. He went to the Emergency Room, then to the intensive medical unit to get stabilized, and finally to the eating disorders unit. Only then did his life begin to change. But in the first family session, Mom and Dad were so timid, they made a shy puppy look aggressive by contrast.

Jim, the family therapist, welcomed the Eggersons for the first visit. One look at how Eggie turned his fury on his parents told it all. Mom and Dad were walking on eggshells. "Folks, I look forward to working with you. Anorexia is a tough illness, but Eggie has the potential to get completely better, especially with parents who are willing to work with us. But the first thing you have to do is stop walking on eggshells. You are scared to death you'll do the wrong thing. You are blaming yourselves. You're afraid you've caused this. You are worn out, worried, exhausted. It not your fault. It's no one's fault. You have to stop worrying you'll say or do the wrong thing."

Mom and Dad couldn't believe it. They took a cautious deep breath. This was so new to them. "But, he always reacted so badly if we didn't do exactly what he wanted; we don't want to make him worse."

Jim replied, "Inside, Eggie desperately needs you—to love him, to set reasonable rules and boundaries, and to bring him to treatment when he is this sick, even if he doesn't see the need. Part of this illness is that Eggie doesn't realize there's a problem. He may call you to say he is being mistreated or we're making him fat, He may want you to take him out of treatment, but don't. And in the meantime, I'd like to assign you some homework: Go to dinner, see a movie, just the two of you, no talk about Eggie until you come back in two days for the next session. And, keep those eggshells in the egg carton, not under your feet."

Comment

Parents of an eating disordered teen often become worried and overly cautious about everything they say. It is almost as hard for them to act normally, and not make their Eggies the center of all their thoughts and actions, as it is for the child to change. They need to practice normal, healthy, balanced behaviors and thinking, just like Eggie will learn to do. That's where family therapists come in. No more walking on eggshells. Normal, healthy, balanced lives for parents and for their eating disordered son. What a relief!

Originally published in 2004.

78

Chasing Up the Wrong Tree

family dynamics, magical thinking, relationships

Spot the beagle, loved to chase squirrels. One day, when he went out for his early morning constitutional, Spot saw two squirrels, each sitting in a different pine tree in the backyard. One squirrel, let's call him Sam, sat high up in the pine tree on the left side of the yard. The branch Sam was sitting on was way up there, at least twenty feet above the ground. He sat contently, polishing his nails, and running floss through his teeth to clean them after eating the last breakfast nut.

The other squirrel, Steve, sat in the pine tree on the right. The branch Steve was sitting on was wide and low to the ground, only three feet from the ground. Steve the squirrel was happily thinking of all the nuts he had hidden for the oncoming winter, whistling an annoyingly cheerful tune, while daydreaming of the hidden nuts. While he whistled, he swung his bushy tail back and forth to keep time.

After thinking for a while, Spot made his decision. He charged the pine tree on the left, trying time and time again to reach Sam, who sat way above. Sam knew that the beagle couldn't possibly jump that high. Spot occasionally looked at the pine tree on the right, the one with Steve the squirrel sitting only three feet from the ground, but remained focused on Sam. Spot scratched and jumped. He yelped in frustration. Even after taking another glance to the right, he kept trying to get to Sam, until he was totally exhausted. Spot the beagle never reached the squirrel sitting high up in the pine tree on the left.

Comment

Some people keep trying for the relationship they would like to have, and fantasize about what it could be like, even when it may be with someone who is least likely to respond. For example, a daughter might crave the love and connection of an absentee parent. A girl might want to date a boy who has no interest in her. A guy might want to be friends with someone incapable of friendship. We can help patients who are like this to recognize that they will be healthier and happier by spending time and energy forming a wide network with non-troubled friends and family members. Striving for the unattainable is a fantasy.

Let's help folks to stop chasing up impossible trees, teach them how to practice communication skills, and help them work through the fantasies of the impossible relationship. Instead, encourage them to make many good relationships with the many "squirrels" on low hanging branches.

Originally published in 2005.

79

Answer the Phone! The Doorbell is Ringing!

bulimia, binge eating, people pleasing, recovery tool

Susie was settling in for a pleasant supper with her boyfriend. They planned to go to a movie later. As soon as she and Joe started to eat, the phone rang. "Better answer it," she said. Five minutes later, having finally said to the telemarketer that she had to go, she sat down again. "Salesmen! They should know people are having supper at this time." Joe did a slow burn but didn't say anything.

Joe reached across the table and took Susie's hand. "Susie, this is a delicious casserole. Where is it from?"

"Joe, I found it in a cookbook that one of my... Rats! Sorry, gotta get the door." Joe could hear part of the conversation. "Great to see you guys. I've already ordered a case of oranges from the dance team at school. I see you're representing the men's gymnastic team. Well, I suppose I could use another crate. Let me get a check."

Ten minutes later, Susie took her place at the table. "You know Joe, I can't decide whether to see that animated film that's supposed to be so cute or should we go to that new comedy... hold on, I'm sorry. This blasted phone is ringing again. It'll just take a minute."

"Hi Aunt Jen. Great to hear from you. No, I'm not busy. Uh huh, that's good, it was just constipation.... Really! How is Uncle Ted? Oh, no. Sorry to hear about that... The weather? It's not too bad here ..." Ten minutes later, the food was cold. "It will only take a minute to heat this up."

"I can't believe it," she said, checking her cell phone, "It's Mom. It must be important. Let me step into the other room and make this as quick as possible." And so on, and so on. The cycle of interruptions continued—the phone, the doorbell, the buzzer on the dryer.

It was very unusual, but Joe developed a migraine and begged off the movie. "Sue, I'd love to see a movie with you another time. It wouldn't be any fun with this headache. I'll call tomorrow." Strangely though, he didn't. Susie felt confused about why she binged on ice cream and pizza after Joe left, and then felt so sick and guilty she purged. But she thought that if she skipped breakfast the next morning, that would make up for the binge. She was even more confused when the salad at lunch turned into a double fudge sundae, followed by two cheeseburgers and double fries. Of course, she had to purge.

When she returned home she continued to be puzzled. She was beginning to ask herself the important questions she had learned in therapy to stop a binge. "What is the feeling I have just before the urge to binge? Am I anxious, depressed, angry, bored? Why?" Just as she was beginning to make progress in her thoughts, the phone rang. "I better answer this," she said, "Then maybe I can get back to making sense of my bulimia."

Comment

Urges to binge or purge or restrict *are urges, not commands.* They are only electronic signals, like phones ringing. Phones do not have to be picked up every time they ring. No one will die if the doorbell isn't answered. Let that sense of urgency and vague feeling of guilt die down. The urge to interrupt good stuff and answer these electronic signals will lessen if you ignore them. Get back to eating dinner, holding Joe's hand, and talking about how your day went. But don't interrupt your life for those almost always trivial signals. They are not commands.

Let's help our patients recognize that urges to binge, urges to purge, skipping a meal, that tsunami-strength urge to run ten miles despite the knee pain, *these* are the doorbells ringing. Resist eating disordered behaviors and they will diminish. Wait them out long enough to make sense of your feelings, and choose a healthy alternative.

At a recent combined conference with the National Institute of Mental Health and the National Institute of Drug Abuse, a good study was presented showing a straight line relationship between increased number of family meals eaten together and decreased eating disordered symptoms and behaviors. Uninterrupted family meals, or meals with a friend or significant other, at least five or—better—seven days a week, are highly protective in decreasing substance abuse or eating disorders.

So, draw up the moat. Cut off the signals until you choose to tune back in. Protect yourself. Imagine a protective shield around your personal space and your family meals, choosing your life, not urges. It's fun once you get perspective.

Originally published in 2005.

80

The Family Time Machine

recovery tool, family dynamics, transition to puberty

Do you want to enter a time machine that may change your life? Let's join Chelsea, a modern-day teenager, as she takes a ride into the past.

Time Machine Captain: "Fasten your seat belt. Approaching take off. The landscape is going to move fast. You may get dizzy. OK. Here we go."

Chelsea: "Look at that little kid, he just burped up his supper on his nice new playsuit. Look at that diaper. He really needs to be changed. Did you see the way he threw the spinach at the wall. Oh, no. He's angry. He's doing his 'hold your breath until you turn blue routine' so his mom and dad will never feed him that green slime again. I used to do that too. Wait minute. I think I recognize him. That nose! Those eyes! Unbelievable—that baby is Dad!"

Captain: "Hold on. The time machine is going to hop ahead."

Chelsea: "He is so cute reciting that poem at the school play. Those old people are my grandparents. They are clapping so hard. He's going backstage. Jake and Kirk just punched him in the stomach and called him a fatty…. Now I can see him in a high school classroom. The teacher is saying he is dumb and fat. He's thinking inside he wishes the teacher knew that the letters are mixed up in his mind. He had dyslexia, but no one knew it! He's crying. I've never seen him cry. Maybe that's why he tells me I have to buckle down and study so hard.

"You know, I've only seen Dad as a grown up—go to work every day, come home and walk the dog, jog five miles no matter what, stare at the TV. This is truly amazing, he's looking under his arm and wondering where those hairs came from. Ugh!"

Captain: "Do you want to go back further?"

Chelsea: "Hey, that's my grandparents, when they were first married, living in a dinky little apartment with Grannie's three sisters and her parents. Wow, and with only one bathroom! That radio belongs in a museum and there is no TV. Poor great-aunt Sally—she is wearing a hand-me-down dress with patches. She looks so proud. I wouldn't wear that unless it was Halloween. Gee, they have an 'icebox'—and there are glass bottles of milk at the front door with cream on top.

"Dad never talked much about his father, but I never could figure out why. My grandfather is writing a note saying he is a failure—he can't support the family or find a job. He has a gun! He fired it. There are brains all over. I've seen horror films, but this is worse, get me out of here."

Captain: "How about a look at your mom when she was a teenager? It's much prettier—sort of."

Chelsea: "Mom really is beautiful. She has wavy hair and big brown eyes, just like me. She's combing her hair a fifth time, waiting for the phone to ring. It's one of those old-fashioned black ones with a rotary dial. I can hear her answering, 'Sure, Jim. Eight o'clock is good. I'll see you at my house.'

"It's eight o'clock. The bell is ringing. Looks like Mom is making sure she doesn't come across as too eager. She's taking her time to put on another coat of lipstick and blots it carefully. Maybe this will be the night when she gets her first kiss, at least that's what I hear her thinking.

"She is really nervous but doesn't want to show it. This is fun, watching her date. They really are having a good time at the ice cream parlor. Oh my God, she's getting her first kiss—how cute—just a little peck on the lips. Oh, good, he asked her out for another date. Maybe some people back then did have a good time. I never knew Mom could be nervous—she seems so controlled and organized all the time."

Captain (after returning to the Here and Now with only a small jolt on landing): "You can learn a lot by taking a ride in the time machine. You may not think about it much, but your parents had parents. They went through all the parent-kid stuff, too, and it wasn't any easier for them. Get them to talk about their past. Ask them what it was like when they were young. Also, ask your grandparents what it was like when they were kids. They are a living history, and you'll feel much closer to them."

Comment

Whether parents and teen kids interact reasonably through the speed bumps of adolescence, or are having a tough time arguing about all the things parents and teens argue about—homework, curfew, chores, allowance, friends, clothes, hair, make-up, going out, hooking up, drugs—inviting parents to share what it was like when they were young always brings more closeness. You can better understand why they say what they say, and their beliefs, quirks, fears, demands, joys, and passions.

In *The Dance of Anger,* Harriet Lerner suggests this approach to breaking through chronic anger with parents—asking them about how they got to where they are; what their parents were like—back then—not now. If our patients can get to know more about their parents and whole extended family (in person or through diaries), life will be richer and make more sense. Every family tree has a rich array of characters that contribute to the heritage of those who are alive. Our time machine combines letters, diaries, pictures, and movies. Get your family members to share their life experiences, and then pass on your own journey.

Originally published in 2005.

81

Let's Play the Blame Ball Game

anorexia nervosa, family dynamics, males

Aaron and Bobby sat down for supper. Mom hadn't come home from work yet, and Dad was cooking supper. Aaron started off the predictable dialogue, "Bobby, you really blew it on the pitcher's mound today. You couldn't get one over the plate to save your life. It's your fault that the Tigers lost."

Bobby responded, "I wouldn't be so stressed out if you hadn't been so stupid and lost forty pounds for the wrestling season, that's why my pitching was off today."

"That was my coach's idea not mine. He's the one to blame for telling me to take off a few pounds."

"Getting in shape and taking off a few pounds is fine, but what you did was insane. It was your fault, not the coach's," Bobby said.

Mom arrived home from work, and the family sat down to eat. The O'Reillys tried to have supper together once in a while, but the kids' schedule and Mom's work wouldn't let them do it regularly. "Well, guys," Mom said, "How's it going?"

Aaron piped up first, "Bobby's pitching really sucked today."

Bobby wouldn't let that remark pass. "Aaron, I haven't been able to sleep lately—your weight loss has stressed out everybody. If you hadn't gotten yourself into that anorexia stuff, we'd all be a lot better. That was really dumb."

"I think the problem is deeper," Dad interjected. "Aaron has been skipping mass and hasn't been saying his prayers regularly. When you stop practicing your spiritual life, bad things are bound to happen."

Mom thought for a moment, and then said to Dad, "You might be right. But you haven't looked hard enough for a real job, and that's being a bad role model for the kids. Maybe Bobby didn't pitch well because he doesn't work hard enough. Also, it is a little embarrassing to have a brother with anorexia nervosa; I thought only girls got this problem. Maybe he's not quite got this becoming a man stuff figured out."

Dad was fuming, "Your comment makes me furious. You take your work much more seriously than our home life. We always come in last place as far as your attention is concerned. If I got a little more respect and affection, maybe I'd have a job and our kids wouldn't be screwed up."

"What do you mean screwed up, Dad?" asked Bobby. "Every pitcher has a day off. I'm sick and tired of being blamed when we don't win."

Aaron reacted to Mom's comment, "That's really mean about my not figuring out about becoming a man. I used to date Mary Jo before the coach made me lose all that weight. Now, I just don't feel like it any more."

"Like I said," offered Dad, "if you both took your religious life more seriously, you'd be in better shape."

The O'Reillys went off to their weekly family therapy session. Dr. Frank invited the family in and let them pick their seats. He noticed they spread out as far as possible but let it pass. "So how's the family doing this week?"

Dad spoke first, "Well, we've been getting nowhere with Aaron. He says he *can't* gain weight, but I think he *won't*. I believe if he connected more to spiritual life, he'd be just fine."

"Dad, that's a lot of crap," said Aaron.

Mom quickly jumped in, "Aaron, we don't talk that way in our family. You're picking up bad language from those kids you hang out with. I think you're not getting better because you don't want to—you really haven't been working at it."

"Aaron's stupid anorexia is stressing out the whole family," added Bobby.

"Let's slow this down a bit, folks," said Dr. Frank. "I see a lot of blame going around. You know, the blame ball is being thrown around like a hot potato. It sounds like each of your is blaming someone else for your choices. Aaron tosses the blame ball to Bobby, saying he should be blamed for losing the game. Aaron tosses the blame ball for his illness to everyone else. Mom blames Dad for not living up to her image. Dad blames Mom for doing what more than half of the Moms in this country do—going out to work. Here's the truth, and it may take you a while to get used to it. No one is to blame for anything that's going on.

"All pitchers have an off game now and then. Dad could not predict that his company would downsize. Mom going to work is fine and normal, and the unpredictable hours go with the territory." Everyone was silent, intensely trying to digest the idea that no one has to be blamed.

Finally, Dr. Frank brought up Aaron. "Anorexia nervosa is the same illness, whether a guy or a girl develops it. By the way, it has nothing to do with not liking girls. Huge weight loss naturally diminishes sexual drive and dating interest. So, I'd like you all to let this sink in, because it's true. No one is to blame for Aaron's anorexia nervosa.

Dr. Frank picked up an imaginary ball, "This is the blame ball, and I'm going to throw it out the window. No one is to blame. Until we get rid of playing the blame game, we won't be able to make progress." He then walked over to the window and tossed it right out the window. Then, they were able to get on with real therapy.

Comment

So often, the unquestioned supposition is that someone has to be blamed for eating disorders, and the hunt is on to find that person or situation. Not only is this assumption wrong, but it's harmful and distracts from getting on with effective treatment. There are the usual suspects: the overbearing mother, physically and emotionally distant father, images of thin movie stars in the media, genes. These assumptions are wrong! Often, the first step in effective therapy is tossing the blame ball out the window.

Originally published in 2006.

82

Run by the Numbers

recovery tool, all ED, mirrors and scales, quality of life

Thebe was on her way home from the moon of Jupiter, which had been named after her to settle a dispute over space rights in the asteroid belt. Unfortunately, she started running out of liquid hydrogen and helium for her spaceship and was forced to land on a planet she had never visited, but had learned about in intergalactic school. The planet Gea (locals called it "Earth") was green and blue, but had been getting grayer and grayer over the last centuries. She did not know whether there was intelligent life there.

She brought her spaceship to a halt in a suburb of Indianapolis and stopped at the first house to ask where she could find compressed helium and hydrogen. Luckily, the man who answered the door was a chemist and gave her directions to a nearby supply house. But before she left, she noticed something strange. A man was being pushed down the street in a wheelbarrow filled with a four foot high green sign that read "$100,000." As he passed by, she heard him say, "Gotta' bill more hours this week or I'll never make $100,000 this year."

Before she could think what this strange activity meant, she saw a very slim, attractive young woman, about 15 years old racing down the street pushing a five foot tall scale. If she slowed down, the scale's extended hands pushed her to go faster. Thebe could see there was a large, red arrow pointing to the number 99, and all the higher numbers were in the "Danger Zone."

Thebe's gills were working faster and faster to adjust to the gray air, and she wondered if her mind was playing tricks on her when more strange things happened. A muscular young man of 17 years was being poked and prodded by a large wooden baseball bat. On its side were carved the numbers .350 followed by the words "failure not allowed." As he ran down the street swinging two regular size bats in front of him, Thebe heard him muttering "Gotta' have a .350 batting average or I'll be a failure again. Harder, harder, swing harder, you wimp."

On Jupiter, Thebe's mother had been very kind, with reasonable standards, and was very supportive of Thebe's goal of being an intergalactic peace practitioner, so all of this push and shove and being run by numbers was very confusing, to say the least. Thebe thought she would chat with a mother who was hurrying her children off to school. The woman wore a stopwatch the size of a Jupiterian rock turtle attached to her wrist. She said to Thebe, "What do you want. I'm behind already, and the day hasn't started yet. I got up seven minutes late, so I hope this is important."

Suddenly, her watch blurted out a loud message, "Time is money. You are wasting time. Hurry. You have two minutes to finish the next four items on your To Do List!" The mother suddenly dropped down to the ground and did ten sit-ups, quickly jumped up, and ran away.

Thebe found the place with the compressed liquid hydrogen and helium and prepared her spaceship for takeoff. All around her were people briskly moving about with signs like: "Zero Calories," "Size 2," "Get 18-Inch Biceps."

Thebe observed, "What a weird place this Gea is. On my planet, and every other one I know of in the solar system, the inhabitants run numbers, they don't run us. I can't get out of here fast enough." With that she floored the accelerometer and zoomed away.

Comment

When you think of it, how many people aren't run by numbers, especially our eating disordered patients. It's all about weight, percentage body fat, miles run, calories burned, GPA, dollars per hour, and sit ups. It's exhausting when you think about it.

Numbers only have the power we give to them, but it's disastrous when they run our lives. Take the power back from them and watch them collapse. It works. It feels better. Cheers and good luck.

Originally published in 2006.

83

Lasso That Calf

all ED, recovery tool, therapy

Zeke was a true cowboy. One beautiful late spring day, he started to herd a hundred fast-growing, young cattle from their birth ranch north to Summer Meadows, where they could graze on the greenest grass in the West. Zeke looked like a cowboy. He sat comfortably in a saddle for hours at a time. His horse, Prince, worked like he was born to it. Zeke had on his jeans and chaps, his sheepskin vest and spurs. His hat was beaten up and sweat stained, but shaded his deep brown eyes.

"Let's move, Prince," he said, and started to herd the frisky cattle. Things didn't go smoothly. First one, then another calf darted to the west, right down into Yester Year Valley. Then at least three calves made a break for Tomorrow Gulch toward the east. Darn if he couldn't catch them. No sooner had he wiped his forehead when a few more young cattle headed out of reach into Yester Year Valley. It went like this for days, losing calves each day either to Yester Year Valley or Tomorrow Gulch. When he arrived at Summer Meadows, only a dozen calves were delivered to the old foreman, Bud.

"Bud, I am unbelievably sorry for what happened. I just couldn't catch those frisky calves when they darted away. I'll make up for the cost from my next job. But what should I do? You're an old hand on the range with years of herding. What's the secret, Bud?"

"Well, Zeke, it's simple. And don't blame yourself. We all lose calves to Yester Year Valley and Tomorrow Gulch. What you need is a lasso and some lessons on lassoing those calves. Here's what you do. The moment that calf breaks, circle that lasso over your head like, "I'm gonna' show you!" Rope that calf and gently bring him back to the herd. Then you'll deliver 100 out of 100 to Summer Meadows."

So Bud showed Zeke how to lasso calves. First, he made a circle of the right weight rope. Then he gave Zeke lots of encouragement as Zeke tried to lasso a fence post, then a calf in a corral, and then a frisky calf on the range. Soon Zeke had his skills well practiced. "The most important thing, Zeke, is to notice right away when a calf is darting to Yester Year Valley or Tomorrow Gulch. Then, quick as a rattler, you gently throw that lasso around the calf, stop him in his tracks, and bring him back to the herd."

The next herding went much better. Zeke had to keep his eyes focused on the trail ahead most of the time. But with his peripheral vision, he got better and better at noticing whenever a frisky young calf started to run toward Yester Year Valley or Tomorrow Gulch. No more calves lost. All of them got to Summer Meadows. Yup, every one. Zeke never forgot Bud's lessons on tossing that lasso and pulling those calves back on the trail. Soon Zeke became a cowboy legend. If you look closely about sunset near Snowy Range, especially in late spring, you will see Zeke lassoing those calves and steering them ahead to Summer Meadows.

Comment

So many eating disordered patients, especially those with anorexia nervosa, spend the majority of their day trying to re-do the past, or trying to anxiously anticipate all the problems that the future might bring. The result is that there is precious little time and energy for the Here and Now, the only time and place where anything productive can be done.

When I have asked patients to keep a record of whether their thoughts were in the past, present, or future, the record usually showed that at least two-thirds of the time, their thoughts were in the Guilty Past or Anxious Future, not Here and Now.

Necessary planning for the future, for example, finding out what courses are needed for a college major, is not anxious anticipation. But future thinking usually focuses on problems. Anxiety is essentially a pervasive sense of inefficacy in handling what is coming up. Also, almost every worry about the future is far out of proportion to the reality—mostly ordinary things will happen. If the unexpected should happen, take care of it.

Asking patients to visually lasso those thoughts that dart into the past and the future and gently bring them back to the trail may help them more than an abstract suggestion to be in the present. Like any skill, getting the idea is not enough. It has to be practiced. Gently and patiently lasso those thoughts and bring them back to Here and Now.

Originally published in 2006.

84

Holidays from the Inside Out

quality of life, recovery tool

Sarah, Mary, and Abrihet were getting together after all of their holidays had been celebrated—Chanukah, Christmas, and Kwanza—to tell each other about the fun they'd had. Buds since grade school, they gathered at Abrihet's house during the Winter break from junior high.

Sarah started the conversation. "On each day of the eight days of Chanukah, we receive a present. I have gotten so good at telling what is inside by looking at the outside—I just know from the way a present is wrapped, how big it is, how heavy it feels, what is going to be inside. Of course, I try to look surprised, and I am almost always happy about the gift."

Mary couldn't believe what she was hearing—it gave her courage to share with her best friends her own inner ability, which she had kept quiet about. "I, well, I don't know how to say this, and you've got to tell me you won't say I'm freaky, but I could actually see inside the gift boxes that were under the tree at Christmas. It felt weird, but I saw there was a new iPod, that small one you can carry anywhere, and I saw the pearl earrings from my grandmother. I didn't even have to guess from the outside wrapping what was inside. I could see the goodies inside like I had x-ray vision. Is that weird or what?"

Abrihet was stunned. She said, "I'm not surprised at all. People have all sorts of abilities that they rarely tell anyone. We had a great time celebrating Kwanza—I guess I'm an African-American now, or really a Nigerian-American, since my parents came here for school and never left. Grandma Dela o Konde finally came to live with us last year. Now, this is what I'm getting to: I can see the insides of people—what is in their stomach, whether they have a kidney stone, or if there is a bad disc in their back, even gross stuff, like if they need a laxative. It all comes rushing into my mind, like that movie where a family gets shrunk and jets around the body through the blood vessels. I don't know what to do with this ability."

It was only because they were such good friends that they dared to talk about their unique abilities. Even though they thought they were whispering, Grandma Dela o Konde couldn't help overhearing them. She came into the living room dressed in her festive holiday Nigerian robe and sat down quietly beside the girls. "Don't worry, kids (her English was very good because she went to a bilingual, parochial school in Nigeria), we each have special gifts. Do you want to hear about mine?"

"You bet," said Sarah. Mary nodded.

Abrihet first felt embarrassed, then looked proud, and said, "Yeah, Grandma Dela o Konde, tell us. You are such a wonderful person. This has got to be something special."

So Grandma Dela o Konde told them about her special gift. "You know, my name in Nigerian means, a girl who is born after many brothers. My parents thought they would never have a girl, and then, finally, I was born. Not only that, I was given a special inner gift from my own grandmother, Amachi. She gave me the capability to see inside of people—not what they had for lunch, although there's nothing wrong with that. Not what's inside of a gift box, like Mary's way or Sarah's way. No, she gave me the gift to see inside of other people's hearts. I can see inside your heart, Sarah. This was a tough Chanukah, the first without your grandfather. There are a lot of beautiful smiles on your face, but there's a kind of hole inside of your heart. It will heal, because your grandfather gave you so much love and fun times that he will live inside of you forever." Sarah cried, then she smiled and hugged Dela o Konde.

"Mary, I can see that you are proud you were able to stop the binge-purge cycle when you felt helpless only a couple of months ago. That is a real accomplishment, even if you are shy about sharing it. You have lots more, in addition, to be proud of, especially the wish in your heart to make the new neighbors from Guatemala feel at home on the block. Why not let others see the beauty that is inside of you. You have so much beauty inside"

"Abrihet, no, I'm not going to criticize you or tease you for seeing what people had for lunch, but you better not let Mrs. Appleby know you could see that extra bar of chocolate she ate when she thought I wasn't looking. Try looking a little deeper, Abrihet, beyond the biology of the person you are looking into. And, by the way, if the local MRI machine at the hospital breaks down, you could be in for a nice paying job!"

"Actually, for all three of you, there's something else that means a lot to me. I want to give the gift that my grandmother gave me—to be able to see inside the hearts of people. Even though I've been here only a year, I can't believe how so many people judge others by their outsides: their weight, their clothes, how new their car is. I hear people thinking things like, "she's getting so fat," or, "he's really letting himself go with that potbelly," or, "that dress is last year's and she's pretending it's new." Of course, to the person, they are phony, smiling, and giving compliments. In this country, almost every magazine says you have to be thin, thin, thin, or else you're unattractive and a failure. This is not what life is about, girls.

"What I want to give to you, if you will accept it, is the treasure of seeing what is inside people: the love, beauty, and hope that lives in the hearts of others—even if they may act upset, rude, judgmental, or selfish on the outside. You will be able to see who is hurting, who is lonely, who needs a kind word. Even when they say the only thing they want for the holidays is to be thin, you will be able to see that they really want to be accepted, to be less scared of growing up, to be able to be their real selves with others. You can be the first one to accept them as they are. You see, this is my last Christmas. Don't ask how I know, but I know. May I give my gift to you?"

The girls all nodded yes, but couldn't really speak. Then, one by one, Dela o Konde gave them a warm hug; and then, very gently, she placed her hands for a moment on their heads. Finally, she held their hands inside of hers.

"In Nigeria, we say that beauty is not sold and eaten, but our thoughts and dreams are the foundation of our being. Now, you too can look and see in other people—their hopes, dreams, fears, and true desires. You can give the love they need just by being yourselves, and letting them be themselves. So I leave you now with peace in my heart.

You are all my children—not only Abrihet, but also Sarah and Mary. Would you honor me, Sarah, by letting me give you an additional African middle name? It is Isoke, which means "a beautiful gift from God." And Mary, I'd like to add Akanke as another middle name. Akanke means "to meet her is to love her." From now on, sure you're normal teen girls and all that, but also, you now have the gift of seeing how people look from the inside out, not having to guess from the outside in."

And with that she vanished into a graceful spiral of perfumed air, quietly saying "Inshallah." When their amazement wore off, the girls noticed there in the air was a very subtle fragrance, which had hints of *coctu spectabilis,* the Nigerian national flower, a bit of wild rose, and a touch of banana.

Comment

Happy Holidays.

Originally published in 2006.

85

Three's a Crowd

all eating disorders, family dynamics, recovery tool, relationships

Amanda dropped a bus token into the fare box as she boarded the municipal bus to the fairground, but the driver stopped her, "What about paying for your companion?"

Amanda looked confused. She turned to her right and then to her left, and said to the driver, "What companion?"

The man frowned, "The one beside you." Amanda shrugged her shoulders, but he was insistent. "Either pay up or get off the bus." So, despite her bewilderment, she threw a second token into the box and sat down by herself.

She wanted to cheer herself up by going to the county fair that was in town for the week. She looked over all the rides and decided to take a chance on the stomach turning twirling ride that spins you overhead in a full 360 degrees while spinning counterclockwise. She bought herself a ticket, gathered her courage, and stepped up to the ticket taker.

He surprised her by saying, "I'm sorry, young lady. Only one person can fit into the seats on this ride."

Amanda was totally bewildered. She complained to the ticket taker "But it's only me. One person, me."

He replied, "Better look again."

"Oh, well," she said, and walked away shaking her head.

Amanda thought that everything had been so confusing today, but she still looked forward to her luncheon date. She met Jan at the restaurant, but when they asked for their table, the hostess said Jan had only reserved a table for two. "I'm sorry. It's real busy. We only have a table for two. Three's a crowd." So, they grabbed some fast food, and Amanda complained about her day.

Later, Amanda had an appointment with Dr. Sandy Stone, her therapist. Amanda collapsed into a chair and moaned, "I don't know what's going on." The bus driver made me pay twice. At the amusement park, the ticket taker said they couldn't fit two people on the wild ride, and at the restaurant, where I met my friend Jan, they said 'Three's a crowd.' What the heck is going on?"

Sandy, who asked patients to call her by her first name, looked with caring eyes at Amanda and said with obvious concern: "Well, Amanda, here's what's going on. You don't have to look in a mirror. You won't see another flesh and blood person. All these people are talking about your eating disorder, which you carry with you everywhere you go. It's really like having another person with you."

They let that sink in for a minute, and then Sandy explained more, "Think about it from your parents' viewpoint. You're having a nice lunch together, you are all enjoying a conversation, but suddenly, you start talking about being fat, right out of the blue. And then you get up and go to the bathroom for ten minutes. After that, you come back and act as if nothing had happened. That is way confusing to others. It's just like having another person with you, a person who is not invited, who is not nice."

Amanda reflected, "Sandy, I feel hurt, but I finally get it. I'm beginning to see what it's like from the eyes of others. I want to be a single, healthy person. Can we get down to work?"

"Sure we can, Amanda. Let's get started. You don't need this extra person. You're plenty good enough by yourself."

Comment:

It can be tough—but necessary—for parents to say to a daughter or son with an active eating disorder that they are welcome but the eating disorder isn't. It's chaos when a child, regardless of age, comes home and practices their eating disorder. It's not good for the sufferer or for the family. Patients begin to get better when they say they realize they "have" a disorder, not that they "are" the disorder. It whispers it's a friend, but it's really an unwanted companion. Let's help them let go of the false friend of the eating disorder.

Originally published in 2007.

86

Where Are You When You Are Eating?

all ED, recovery tool, mindfulness

A group of four high school students were having lunch at the new South-western Grill on a Saturday afternoon. It was a fun restaurant—with real cactus, warm colors, and authentic food.

After the food arrived, John immediately thought back to how his wrestling coach had warned him about getting too fat in the off-season. With mechanical action he ate, but his mind was on wrestling and how hard it is to drop weight. "Hey, get off my case, Coach," he wished he could say, but John couldn't get off his own case. Gun to head, he couldn't say after the meal what he had eaten.

Sue got nervous as soon as she took one look at the tortilla chips and mango salsa the waiter put on the table when they were seated, and once her Santa Fe chicken salad arrived, Sue feared that she would never fit into her prom dress in a few weeks. While her jaws worked, she saw herself trying to squeeze into her beautiful gown, its seams tearing on the dance floor. The image felt so real, she could sense her anger and disgust rising against her hips. Food? What food? The plate was clean, but so was her memory of the meal.

Joan got a plank steak with hot peppers—just the smell generated feelings of anxiety and her mind bounced back to when her boyfriend patted her on the hips and said she was getting a little heavy. Her stomach churned and she could hardly swallow. She thought of all the things she could have said to him but never did, and she barely touched her food.

Brad decided on the house special, which sounded good when the waiter described it to him, but while he was eating, he couldn't remember what it was. His mind was stuck on a script of being teased last week at school. He kept repeating the bully's words and what he'd like to do the guy. The humiliation still tingled in his bones, and it was certainly more real than the flavors of the house special. His body was drenched in sweat, and even with these close friends he was afraid that they were judging him.

When they got together on campus on Monday afternoon, it was funny, sad, and puzzling. None of them could remember what they had for lunch on Saturday. In fact, none of them could remember their morning showers or even what they'd studied in their classes moments earlier. Their minds were everywhere else. They were there, but they weren't there.

Comment

In his 1990 book, *Full Catastrophe Living*, Jon Kabat-Zinn, a pioneer of the powerful therapeutic method of mindfulness, described asking a question of the audience during a lecture, "When you took a shower this morning, where were you?" Almost everyone in the audience smiled. They were all therapists and understood professionally and personally. Even in this group, almost no one was really in the shower, feeling the water, letting it spray over the hair and run down the body in warm rivulets of pleasing sensation. Some were into their schedules for the day. Others worried about yesterday's sessions. One young psychologist rehearsed the anger she had swallowed the day before talking to her supervisor. They may have been in the shower, but their minds weren't.

We can help our patients deal with meals by having them practice here-and-now mindfulness about the process of eating—being present with their feelings, especially the pleasant sensations the body perceives when hunger is satisfied and the pleasure of social interaction that is real not mechanical. When clinicians and therapists first practice being where they are at that moment with full awareness, without judgment, with openness to what thoughts and feelings are going on, they are on their way to helping patients be mindful. Let's help our patients to be really present when they eat—experience taste and scent—letting the past stay in the past, and the future in the future. Being healthy means being aware of and enjoying the sensations of eating in a social context. Be mindful. Help our patients to be mindful.

Originally published in 2007.

87

Of Mirages and Fool's Gold

perfectionism, recovery tool

The two-way Wilderness contest was under way. The time was ideal, late spring in Utah, where the low mountains met the desert. Kevin was to race walk four miles from the starting point at the edge of the desert to a large cactus where a jug of water was waiting for him and then race walk back. Kurt was to pan for flakes of gold in the stream running through the canyon until he found a half-ounce of gold. The one who accomplished his goal first would be the winner.

Kevin started out with his best race walk—no jogging or bending of the knees was the rule. Soon after the one mile mark he saw something attractive off to his right—something much more interesting than a cactus—an oasis of tall trees with a sparkling waterfall leading to what had to be a beautiful lake. "Why bother with reaching a cactus. Who cares about the rules or race. This oasis is much too beautiful to skip." So he changed directions and broke the rules by jogging toward the oasis. After a while he had to slow down because of the heat. Soon he was crawling on his knees toward the oasis. Strange thing—it kept getting further and further away, but it was no less attractive. Because of his low posture, the judges couldn't see him when he disappeared. They found his parched body a day later, too late for recovery.

Meanwhile Kurt started panning for gold in the chilly stream that came down from the mountains between canyon walls. He was excited when he found his first few flakes of gold and put them into the plastic bottle for safekeeping. When he looked up to the canyon walls, he saw something glittering high up, right above the icy ledges. "Why bother with these little flakes. I see a vein of gold up there, about 50 feet up. That's going to make me the winner—and a rich winner." Kurt threw his gold panning sieve on the ground and started climbing the icy cliff. It was slippery to be sure. But the goal was worthwhile—gold was waiting in that cliff. When he had groped his way about forty feet up, he lost his grip. He let go with both of his hands and broke the rule of always having three of four limbs in contact with the cliff. When they found him a few hours later, his concussion was severe, but he survived. What was especially disappointing was the information he got from the race officials when he was fully conscious. "That's Fool's Gold up there on the cliffs, son. Lots of old miners lost their lives during the gold rush in the 1860s when they got impatient with panning for gold. Looks like gold, but ain't worth a plug nickel."

Comment

Grim? Absurd? Tragic? Maybe all of these. Perfectionism is a mirage. It seems so much more tempting than struggling step-by-step in a race walk toward a thorny goal. Sometimes you work hard and all you get is a cactus, but at least it's a real cactus. The problem with perfectionism is that the goal is never reached. It reminds me of the Sirens calling Odysseus to the rocks in the *Odyssey*. Looks so good. Much better than the race walk of adolescence and the messy process of identify formation. But an illusion.

Perfectionism is also Fool's Gold. It glitters and it glistens, but it is always out of reach. Ibsen said we cannot take from people the "Life

Lie" that makes living possible. Perfectionism is a Life Lie—an illusion, an overvalued belief that seems so real, but disappears like a cloud when you grasp for it. Therapeutically, perfectionism is tough to treat. Anna Freud, in *The Ego and the Mechanisms of Defense,* pointed out that immature ego defenses, such as perfectionism, resist change. Patients try to become perfectly relaxed, to become perfectly non-perfectionistic. It doesn't work that way.

You have to cultivate more mature defenses and take the risk of living without the overvalued belief that perfectionism is possible or worthwhile. Life, especially in adolescence, is filled with decisions to be made between the hard work of panning for real gold versus the allure of Fool's Gold. Let's get our patients to go for real races and real gold, not mirages and Fool's Gold. Perfectionism sucks.

Originally published in 2007.

88

Pre-Traumatic Stress Disorder

anxiety, quality of life, all ED

Elle was shaking like a leaf. Her piano recital was still a month away, but all she could think about was what a disaster it would be. She had to walk up in front of a hundred people, play her piece by heart, and look like she was enjoying the ordeal. As she thought about the recital and her piece, she always came to a point where her memory blocked, and she couldn't remember the next several lines in her mental rehearsal. Her blood pressure increased, her face flushed, her heart skipped beats, and she became drenched in sweat. Every little thing reminded her of the upcoming failure and humiliation—a toy piano in the store, a music shop, even any piece of music played on the radio. Maybe she would need to drop out of school; maybe she would move to her grandmother's town. No, she had to tough it out because dropping out of school or moving would be just as humiliating. She steeled herself to the daily mental blocks and the drenching sweats and skipped heartbeats.

For some unexplained reason, when she eventually gave her recital piece, it was flawless and flowed smoothly. The audience applauded warmly. It took several days to stop thinking they were only being polite.

Now she was free to start agonizing about the speech in class next month. This situation reminded her of last year's SAT practice exam. She studied every night for months, going over vocabulary and math problems. She took a Saturday morning prep-course. Elle knew she would fail anyway. She felt guilty about her certain failure and the shame that was inevitable. She felt guilty about taking her parents' money for the worthless course. When she could sleep, which was not often, she had nightmares about getting the lowest score in the class. She cut down her food intake more and more, saying "At least I can do something right." When she finally got to the exam, her weight had dropped 20 pounds. But she hid it with a bulky sweater. During the exam, every question seemed to be a trick. She had eaten nothing for breakfast and felt faint several times. Weeks later the dreaded letter came, she had scored in the upper 10% of the country.

Comment

We all know about Post-Traumatic Stress Disorder (PTSD). Well, Pre-Traumatic Stress Disorder can also be devastating. The agony suffered by a sensitive, perfectionistic person facing unbearably terrible events coming up can leave the person a wreck, whether the fear is reality based (seldom) or the activity would be an ordinary event for most people but gets amplified exponentially by anticipatory anxiety. Let's call this Pre-Traumatic Stress Disorder (Pre-TSD). The individual's solution is often to turn to restrictive eating, developing into anorexia nervosa, or binge-purge behavior.

The situation Elle faced made me think of the reaction of the Algerian soldier in Camus' absurdist novel, *The Stranger*. As he faced the firing squad and the end of life as a certain upcoming event, everything became meaningless, without purpose, without love. All the past became an illusion. To a young person with Pre-TSD, the same terrifying sequence occurs. The fear of the piano recital, of scoring poorly on a test, or giving a speech in class, can feel like facing a firing squad. The brain, in fact, acts as if there is a death sentence, a terrifying tomorrow.

We can help patients to live in the here and now by preparing them to be realists. By using mindfulness, they can tolerate and even be curious about the fears that enter their mind, the anticipatory anxiety and dread. The anticipation is usually much worse than the reality. The final goal is to give a hearty belly laugh to the fears, and gently escort them to the exit door of the mind.

Originally published in 2007.

89

Do Do a Do—Don't Do A Don't

all ED, compulsivity OCD, recovery tool, mindfulness

Kim needed help. She couldn't stop counting the calories in every food she ate. She couldn't stop counting fat grams on every label in the supermarket. "This is nuts," she said. "Don't do this. Stop it! I won't do this silly counting any more. Don't do it." To reinforce her decision she said, "Don't count, don't count, don't count," every time she ate, every time she shopped. For some strange reason, she not only kept counting calories and fat grams, she started to count the number of steps from the bus to her school, and the number of seconds the light stayed red. She counted the number of stars in the sky...well, not quite, but everything seemed to need counting.

Kim was determined to stop. Every time she said, "Don't count," she added a pull on her ponytail. She slapped her hand when she reached for a label to count the fat grams. Exhausted and discouraged, she remembered her Wise Woman Counselor, Mey-Yan, had said to come back to her if things got tough. She called and found out there was time available later that day.

Mey-Yan listened carefully to Kim as she cried and blurted out her problem. "I really want to stop counting, but nothing works."

Mey-Yan asked Kim to take a deep breath and gently dry her eyes with a tissue. "Kim, would you be willing to do an experiment?"

"Yes."

Mey-Yan continued, "Kim, I don't want you to think of a pink polar bear. I don't want you to think of a pink polar bear. I really don't want you to think of a pink polar bear. What are you thinking of right now, Kim, and how do you feel?"

Kim frowned and sheepishly admitted, "I'm thinking of a pink polar bear. I feel like a failure."

Mey-Yan gently explained to Kim what the experiment was about. "Kim, when I keep saying 'Don't think of a pink polar bear,' of course that's all you are thinking about. The harder you try to do a 'don't,' the more you will think of it. It doesn't work. You can't do a 'don't.'"

She paused a moment and then suggested, "Let's try something else. Do think of a gentle flowing stream, sparkling in the sun, with the water glistening as it passes over rocks. Now, what are you thinking about, and how do you feel?"

Kim said, "I'm imagining a stream flowing with sun shining on the water." Kim's shoulders relaxed and she smiled.

Mey-Yan also smiled, "You see, Kim. You can do a do, but you can't do a don't—the mind doesn't work that way. Next time you have a meal, or are picking out some cans of food in the supermarket, chose a "do" to think about. For example, think about how the food will give you energy, how it will taste, and how healthy you will be... and maybe, remember the stream. Be gentle with yourself. Remember to choose a calming and specific "do." Don't doesn't work. You can choose a positive and let go of what's not working. See you next week."

Comment

It's so frustrating for patients with compulsive behaviors or obsessive thoughts. They know the thoughts are not sensible, frankly "crazy" at times, and the same for the compulsive behaviors. Often they try the

"Just say no" or "Don't do that" methods, or they add self-punishing behaviors like pulling their hair or slapping themselves to stop these thoughts and behaviors. The result is frustration, a sense of failure, and intensification of the "Don't" approach, without benefit.

The principle that Mey-Yan used has been proven to be much more helpful. Choose a "do"—a behavior or thought that is incompatible with the undesired behavior. Obsessive Compulsive Disorder has a strong neurobiological component and individuals with those symptoms are laden with anxiety that only intensifies when negative techniques are tried. For example, anxious individuals often tell themselves or are told by others to "just stop being anxious," and of course that makes anxiety worse. If instead, they are taught how to get out of their head and practice relaxing muscle groups one by one, sometimes adding a relaxing mental scene, these behaviors that produce a relaxed muscle state are incompatible with continued mental anxiety. Telling people to "stop worrying" is cruel in a way. Teaching them to relax and choose a thought and behavior incompatible with the unhealthy behavior is kind, effective, and evidence-based by many studies.

Patients with eating disorders often try ineffective negative or punitive behaviors when they are motivated to change their eating disordered patterns. Let's teach them: Do Do a Do, but Doing a Don't Doesn't Work. Funny English, maybe some giggles, but they get it, and it works.

Originally published in 2008.

90

The Hijacking of Top Down by Bottom Up

all ED, anxiety, therapy

Top Down was piloting a small commuter jet to the town of Good Goal in the Land of Peaceful. As he flew at 450 knots per hour, he was amazed this time, and every time, at the beauty of flying, astonished at the blueness of the skies, the fluffiness of the clouds, and the majesty of the rivers and canyons below.

Suddenly, someone broke into the cockpit. It was Bottom Up, his long time nemesis. Bottom Up said, "Put your hands behind your head and get out of the pilot's seat. I'm taking over." Then he slipped handcuffs on Top Down and attached them to the cockpit door so he couldn't move.

Bottom Up slipped into the pilot's seat and took the yoke of the plane. Bottom up turned the plane in all crazy directions. First, he tilted the plane to the left, then to the right. Then, he did a sudden nose up at 35 degrees, far more than the plane was designed to handle. When the engine began to stall, he turned the nose down to re-ignite the plane, making the turn so fast that passengers were flung to the ceiling. Finally, he did a corkscrew and everyone was sick to their stomachs.

Bottom Up did not notice that Top Down had slipped out of his handcuffs. Even though he was trembling and his knees felt weak, Top Down managed to give Bottom Up a karate kick that sent him to the floor, allowing Top Down to put the handcuffs on Bottom Up and secure him to the door. Top Down took a deep breath, sat back down in the pilot's seat, and slowly regained control of the jet. He leveled the plane, stabilizing the flaps, and returned the plane to the original course, heading for Good Goal in the Land of Peaceful.

As soon as Top Down landed, he put in an order for a better lock on the pilot's door and asked for a sensor that would eject out into the sky any unauthorized person who tried to forcibly enter the cockpit. No more hijacks for Top Down.

Comment

Our executive selves and those of our patients are often hijacked by "bottom-up" anxiety (i.e., anxiety that rises from deep inside of ourselves). It is as if the good goals and sensible plans we have are suddenly taken over by anxiety. In the case of eating disordered patients, the result is usually binge-purge or self-starving activity, and sometimes compulsive exercise. My binge-purge patients tell me that a sudden distressed mood, especially anxiety, is their most common trigger for binges. They scratch their heads and look puzzled when they speak of how confusing it is to suddenly do things they don't want to do.

An important part of therapy is helping patients recognize when anxiety is knocking at the "cockpit door" of the mind, about to barge in and take over. It helps to recognize the first knot in the stomach, the tightness in breathing, the lump in the throat, and the dryness in the mouth. They need to give the feeling a name, and then put into action the plans they made for dealing effectively with the crummy feeling. It helps to keep on hand a card listing stress management skills. Some of the techniques that help include being "mindful" of the anxiety and allowing it to be, rather than *trying* to get rid of it, which only makes it worse. Also, they learn to distract, to relax their muscles, to breathe slowly and deeply, and especially to ask what the thought was that kicked off the anxiety, and then challenge that thought for accuracy.

Brain imaging studies have shown that a fearful sensation, such as a glance at a high calorie dish, a scale, a mirror, can go right to the amygdala, the fear center, and trigger the process of bottom up anxiety that takes over the top down executive self control. Anxiety arising from the amygdala bypasses the healthy decision-making ability located in the pre-frontal and frontal cortex, directly activating physiological changes, such as a fast heart beat, sweating, difficulty breathing, and sends out a jet stream of adrenaline. These changes literally hijack the executive or decision making self. We can help our patients by giving them, figurative locks on the cockpit door—quick response skills they can practice. Blue skies ahead. Happy landings.

Originally published in 2008.

91

Follow Your Star

all ED, recovery tool, goal setting, perfectionism

Sam: "Our Day Program for Eating Disorders is close to completion for this group. You've all worked very hard. I'd like to hear what your plans are after the group is over."

Brittany: "I'm excited by all the expectations I have. I expect to be free from my preoccupation with weight. I expect to get a perfect job, and to do it perfectly. My expectation for relationships is to have lots of friends, to never argue again with my family, and to make every day a sunny one for myself and everyone around me. That's the star I'm following."

Ted: "I'm excited too, but my expectations are way different. I expect my life will be all positive thinking, no more negatives. Those urges to binge and purge will all be gone. I expect to exercise with perfect form and moderation; no more of the out of control exercise. My star is sending me strong rays letting me know that I won't fail."

Brynn: "There are going to be a lot of stars in the sky for me, too. My boyfriend tells me that he expects me never to compare myself with others like I used to do. That was the pits—always seeing myself as fat and stupid. Never again. I expect I'll be a perfect French major with my improved concentration. In fact, I'm calling my Star *ma belle étoile*, French for 'my beautiful star.'"

Sam: "I can tell you are all enthusiastic about being free from your eating disorders. You've all worked hard to put anorexia and bulimia behind you. Let me try out an idea and see what you think. I'm going to suggest you follow a different star, one I put in capitals S T A R. To my mind, expectations are demands in disguise. They are recipes for disappointment, not that you mean to do that. There's also some passivity to expectations—A kind of demand that things *should* happen a certain way, or that a certain event *should* occur. What do you think of substituting the S T A R system of *goals* in place of *expectations?*

"Use the S T A R memory trick: S stands for **Specific**—not vague. For example, instead of being a "perfect" student, consider a specific goal like learning 30 phrases of conversational Spanish. That's clear and specific.

"T stands for **Time Limited**—such as, setting a goal of learning 30 phrases of Spanish in 30 days. That gets you out of the having to do it yesterday or never getting around to it.

"The **A** stands for **Achievable**, meaning your goal is reasonable and can be accomplished by normal human beings. Almost anyone can learn 30 phrases of Spanish, as opposed to being a perfect Spanish student. Perfection isn't achievable.

"The **R** stands for **Ratable**—the goal can be measured, not judged. Are you able to learn all of the phrases or some. Compare that with the un-ratable expectation of being a perfect language student. So, now you can have a goal of 30 phrases of Spanish in 30 days, a specific, time-limited, achievable and ratable goal that will be satisfying to accomplish.

"The neat thing about goals is that they can be changed when it's appropriate. They're flexible. They can be modified to add more or less, to speed them up, or slow them down. There's only a learning experience, no demands in disguise. See you for the final session next week."

Comment

So many of our patients have perfectionistic traits and suffer from unreasonable expectations that make them see themselves as failures. Expectations are seldom achievable and usually reflect all-or-none reasoning. What a recipe for disappointment and failure. Saying, "I expect never to argue with my parents again," is like expecting warm weather in January in Iowa. Sometimes it happens, but don't expect it. You'll be very disappointed. Be a STAR instead.

Originally published in 2008.

92

Halt Bad Dog

bulimia, recovery tool, binge eating

It kept lunging at her. Tamara felt like she was being attacked by a bad dog. The attack continued relentlessly. She placed her hands on her throat for protection. "How did I get myself into this position? I swore it would never happen again. I said I'd never let myself get this vulnerable." All she could think of was running away. But she knew from past experience that it would follow her wherever she went. She couldn't outrun it. Running didn't help. She'd like to call a friend, but there wasn't time. The assault grew stronger. Her breath grew very rapid and shallow. She knew she couldn't avoid it any longer. So she opened the freezer, took out the quart of macadamia nut ice cream and swallowed it in chunks as fast as she could. Then came the last of the brownies.

Her mother called out to her, "What's wrong Tamara?"

"Nothing, mom. I had the crazy idea I was being attacked by a bad dog."

"That's silly, Tamara," her mother said. "Rover never attacks anyone. He would give his hot dog to a burglar."

"Yes, Mom, I know."

In her weekly session, Tamara explained to Kay, her therapist, how it felt. "The attack got stronger and stronger, and I wanted to say 'Stop,' but it didn't stop." Kay gently told Tamara that she had indeed suffered an attack, a binge-attack, built on the concept of a dog attack to help Tamara get it.

"Tamara, let's think of your binge urges as attacks by a bad dog. And then let's stop them by saying 'Halt Bad Dog.'"

"Kay, that's sounds nuts."

"Yes, Tamara, but here's what I mean. Most binge urges, like alcohol urges, occur when a person feels crummy. The alcohol rehabilitation counselors have taught many alcohol-abusing clients to say 'HALT' when they have an urge to drink. That's a shorthand way of saying 'Are you **Hungry, Angry, Lonely,** or **Tired,**' four of the biggest triggers for an alcohol binge. Asking yourself which specific feeling you have as soon as the binge urge starts allows you to deal directly with the trigger and stop it. You have learned in therapy to practice specific, different, approaches when you are hungry, or angry, or lonely, or tired. I'm going to suggest you not only say "HALT" to stop the dog in its tracks, but say "HALT BAD DOG!"

"You know the **HALT** feeling words. Continue the mnemonic: **BAD** stands for **Bored, Anxious,** or **Depressed. DOG** stands for **Demoralized, Overwhelmed,** and **Given up.** The moment you feel the craving for a binge start, visualize it as a bad dog attacking, say 'HALT BAD DOG.' Then deal directly with whichever feeling is asking for a pseudo-solution through a binge—the bad dog attack really is halted. Try it, Tamara."

Comment

The phrase HALT has been used with alcohol abusing clients for some time. It applies just as well to binge urges. Frank, my co-therapist and expert social worker, and I, decided in our group to try out a more complete phrase: HALT BAD DOG. The key is getting a patient to inhibit the binge response for just a little while so that while sitting on the urge, there is enough time to give the dysphoria a name. Our patients then use the different approaches they have learned for different types of emotional distress. They can carry 3x5 cards with each letter and corresponding word of the Halt Bad Dog. Instead of bingeing, they can look through the cards to give their feelings a name. This gives power to the patient to know these attacks can be slowed down, held off, and then avoided completely. Try it. Ruff. Ruff.

Originally published in 2009.

93

The 5:36 Express from Paddington Station

all ED, anxiety, recovery tool, mindfulness

Paddington Station was as busy as usual, with commuters rushing to their train compartments to head for home. London was grimy, and soot filled the air. It would be oh so pleasant to return to the countryside for a long summer evening. As everyone knows from reading Agatha Christie and other British mystery writers, murders take place on the Paddington Express. Today, it was not to be murder, but something else that seemed almost as awful, at least to Jane.

You enter British trains, at least the older ones, directly from the train platform, stepping up through the little swinging doors. Jane briskly entered her compartment and uttered a sigh of relief that she would be alone for the journey, just her and her thoughts, letting the workday slide from her mind with each passing mile. However, as the train was about to leave the platform, a burly man with a handlebar mustache jerked open the door and entered. Oh well, you can't always control those things. But it could be worse than simply having to share a compartment, and it was. The burly man needed a shave and a bath. As soon as the train picked up speed, he pulled out an enormous salami that reeked of garlic. Then, he opened a tin of sardines. Jane was not sure what the last straw was—taking off his shoes and socks to clip his toenails, or spreading out the dirty contents of his suitcase on the vacant seats.

Jane thought about her options? I can kill him and throw him from the train, but I wouldn't want to take someone's life. I could jump from the train myself and hope for the best. That would not be very helpful either. The train must be going 100 km an hour. I could pitch a fit, jump up and down, cry, scream, and glare at him, but the other cabins in the train are probably full, so there is nowhere else for him to go. I suppose I can settle back, read my book, let the unpleasant man be as he is. Then, I will breathe a sigh of relief when he gets off at his stop or when I get off at mine, whichever comes first.

And that is what Jane did on the 5:36 from Paddington Station. The unpleasant man with his inconsiderate behavior, salami, sardines, and nail clippings left the train about halfway to Jane's destination. After Jane aired the cabin out, she pulled out her knitting, settled into a pleasant routine, and enjoyed the remainder of her trip. No murder today on the 5:36 from Paddington. No jumping out of the window of a speeding train. What she needed was patience and the knowledge that she would soon be without her unpleasant companion, because either he would leave first or she would arrive at her station.

Comment

Spells of painful moods (depression, anxiety, boredom, loneliness) all are temporary states, much like the experience Jane had with the unpleasant man in her train cabin. We can help our patients during episodes of dysphoria by asking them to imagine they are on a train ride. Someone very unpleasant enters the cabin and creates an uncomfortable situation—no joke, it's unpleasant to have this jerk on board. But you have to remind yourself that the unpleasant, almost unbearable, person will be getting off the train at his stop or "Jane" (the patient) will be getting off at hers. It's a temporary situation. Knowing that this "person," a metaphor for a painful state of mind, is only short-lived, and really believing that fact, will help a patient to practice mindfulness until it changes or goes away.

The problem comes when a person tries to "murder" that mood state, commit harm to self, becomes desperate about getting rid of the state of mind. These visitors to the cabins of our speeding lives enter without our consent from time to time. They are not pleasant. We validate the fact that they are unpleasant. But we teach our patients that we can tolerate them without taking desperate measures.

In fact, we can go beyond "being with" these states of mind; we can become curious about them. "Now I wonder what caused that person to enter my cabin? What makes him so messy and unpleasant? Maybe he could teach me something if I stopped fuming and asked a few questions, like: Who are you? What brings you here? How long do you plan to ride on the train?"

In the midst of our struggles to separate ourselves from these unpleasant "visitors," we can do things that are much worse than putting up with them. What is most important to remember is that these unpleasant visitors will be leaving the train. Murders on mystery novel trains are okay. Trying to murder temporary mood states is not.

Originally published in 2009.

94

The Most Dangerous Weapon

all ED, teasing, recovery tool

Watch out! It's coming your way. It slashes and it burns. It tears and it scars. There is no weapon in history so terrible. Oh, the war stories that could be told. This weapon has toppled empires in the past. It has caused more damage than all the bones broken in all the centuries since we were hunter-gatherers. What it does to the young and to the old, to the short and the tall, to the tubby and the skinny—well, you can't imagine. Even in your worst nightmare, there is no weapon more savage. Your night-mares may be about this weapon. If you can imagine what a tapeworm does inside of you, what a cobra could do to you, how a meteor falling on your head wallops you, then you need to know this weapon is worse than all of those things.

It is so deceptive. At the very moment you think you can relax, it comes out to assault you. Every sibling owns this weapon. So did that teacher you thought you could trust. In fact, she attacked you in front of the entire class. You were bleeding for weeks. And then there's that "friend." With friends like that, you don't need enemies! She plunged the weapon deep into you when you weren't looking. Would you believe that she posted directions about using this weapon on Facebook and told her "friends" how to get to you?

There are examples of this weapon in all the media, on TV, on the Internet, in the movies, everywhere. Even worse, there are lots of examples of how to use this weapon. Some use it laughingly. But you are the one with the scars and bruises that never seem to heal. Oh my gosh, I don't know how to tell you this, but you have one of these weapons. too. The worst thing I read the other day was that people who were damaged by this weapon might use it on their own children. Maybe I shouldn't have told you that you own a copy of this weapon. Maybe you can figure out yourself what it is.

Comment

"Sticks and stones may break your bones, but words can never hurt you" is 100% incorrect. The exact opposite is true. Bones generally heal quite well. Hurtful words from this weapon—the tongue—may, and often do, last for a lifetime. In vulnerable individuals, the single most common experience that precipitates the onset of eating disorders is a critical comment, especially by parents, siblings, peers, boyfriends or girlfriends, teachers, or coaches. Commonly, a young person starts dieting after hearing dreaded words like "fatty, tubby, stupid" and so, so many others.

When kids are very young, mean words don't seem to have much effect. But they sow seeds to be expressed later. The most obvious time when hurtful words do immediate damage is when young people are forming a personal identity, the challenge of adolescence. Here the concrete has been laid down, but is not set. Words written on this drying concrete stay embedded when the identity is firmed up. The damage can be incredibly hard to undo. You would think the very people who suffered this damage would be more sensitive to their kids, but the opposite is true.

Too often people try to pass off mean, inappropriately critical, ugly words as being of no consequence. I have treated people over 70 years of age who are still struggling with what was said to them when young.

It is important to validate in our patients the fact that words do matter a great deal, and yes, great damage can be done by words even if the speaker says, "I was only joking." Jokes at the expense of other people are forms of sadism. This sadism turns into masochism as the receiver of these words repeats them to herself or himself from a vicious superego. You don't have to use these somewhat older psychiatric terms to understand the terrible damage that can be done by words. The functional MRI shows us that dramatic changes can take place in the brain when certain words are said.

The positive side of this fact is that we can also heal with words. That is why we need to choose them carefully. That is why the book of Proverbs in the Old Testament and other books of wisdom have much to say about words, including the following paraphrases: the speech of destructive people conceals a violent mind; gossip is as sharp and deadly as a sword but the tongue of wise people brings healing; stupid people say dumb and hurtful things; bad words from bad people bring bad results; and finally, tongues have the power of life and death. Whether your source of wisdom is the functional MRI or ancient books of wisdom (try both), it is clear that words have enormous power to hurt or heal. Thankfully, much can be done to pour fresh concrete and write new words of hope and healing in our patients' minds.

Originally published in 2010.

95

Ask the Dry Cleaner

anorexia nervosa, thinness, denial, people pleasing

Meg wanted expert advice for anything important in her life. Her cosmetician always selected the perfect hair color for her. She wouldn't think of changing the arrangement of her living room without guidance from her trusted interior designer, Susie, who had designed the homes of some of the city's best families. Her bike came from a French firm that specialized in titanium bicycles for the Tour de France. Her yoga instructor guided each client with a personal fitness program.

But, Meg had one area in which she was unsure of how to proceed— what should she weigh? Her gynecologist was working with her to figure out why her periods had stopped. Her physician, Dr. Ryan, thought she might be too thin. Meg thought, without saying so, that there was no way she was too thin. After her last visit with the doctor, Meg had a great idea— when she went to pick up her dry cleaning, she would ask Mrs. Lang if she was too thin. Mrs. Lang could remove any spot from any article of clothing. No stain was too tough.

"Mrs. Lang, I was wondering, do you think I am too thin?" she asked the lovely Mrs. Lang. Meg, as usual during cool weather, was wearing a mock turtleneck under an angora sweater, topped by her faux leather coat. "No, dear, I don't think you are too thin. You look beautiful to me," said the dry cleaner.

"Thank you very much, Mrs. Lang. I appreciate your expert opinion." Meg felt reassured. That doctor was an expert in hormones, of course, but couldn't be right about her weight. Not after she heard Mrs. Lang's opinion. It was so important to get advice from the right people.

The comment from her gynecologist that Meg might be too thin still bothered her a bit. So, she asked the UPS delivery woman about her weight. Rae Lynn was a wonderful delivery person. Every shipment was placed neatly by the front door. She was seven months pregnant but did not want to stop the job she loved until the 9th month. "No dear," said Rae Lynn, "you don't look too thin to me. I wish I looked like you but that's the way it goes with pregnancy. You'll know some day."

Dr. Ryan insisted Meg see a specialist at the hospital's eating disorders clinic. She did so in order not to displease Dr. Ryan, but knew it was a waste of time. At the clinic, after a thorough evaluation, they said to Meg, "We believe you meet criteria for an early diagnosis of anorexia nervosa. You have lost too much weight. You are too thin for your age and height." Meg hesitated for a moment and then replied, "You know, that is not possible. I have gotten opinions from two experts who say I am not too thin. Thank you for your time, but I'll be leaving now."

Meg knew what she was doing and what she wanted. She lined up appointments with her interior designer, her colorist, her dermatologist, and several other experts. As she was making these appointments, she thought to herself, "That's so silly, that idea from the eating disorders clinic. I know I am fine in my weight. After all, Mrs. Lang and Rae Lynn told me I am not too thin." Meg always went for expert advice when she needed it.

Comment

How many times have we seen patients who would never go to their stylist or dry cleaner for advice about heart disease or diabetes but think that anyone who says their weight is fine is accepted as an expert? Anorexic thinness in young women is almost always ego-syntonic. The cognitive distortion of filtering is alive and well—any opinion that does not agree with her perceptual distortion that she is just fine gets filtered out, regardless of whether that opinion is from a parent, physician, or psychologist.

Sometimes, when I share the opinion, based on evaluation, that a young woman has early anorexia nervosa, and she says others think she is fine, I reply, "Well, let's ask the plumber about your hair color and the bakery owner about your interior design, how about it?" The reply is "No, of course not. That's silly, I want experts to advise me." Our normative cultural distress is so common that many women believe that "normal" weight is achieved only when she is at least 15% *below* her ideal body weight. We have to use motivational techniques to help women accept truly expert help about weight.

Originally published in 2010.

96

AH HA

cognitive behavioral therapy, all ED, recovery tool

Sylvia: "I'm no good at anything."

Babs: "AH HA."

Sylvia: "Wish you would stop saying that."

Babs: "HA HA."

Sylvia: "At least it's a nice day out. The sun is finally breaking through the clouds."

Babs: "You bet. Love it."

Sylvia: "I don't think anyone likes me."

Babs: "AH HA."

Sylvia: "That is so annoying."

Babs: "Yes, probably is."

Sylvia: "Did you catch the last episode of *Glee*?"

Babs: "Sure did. What a great show. Would you believe a show about a school glee club would be a big hit. Can't wait for each episode."

Sylvia: "I look like a frumpy cow."

Babs: "AH HA, HA HA."

Sylvia: "You know, sometimes you are so normal and sometimes you are so weird."

Babs: "You are probably right."

Sylvia: "Why is it we can have a decent conversation sometimes and then you start sounding like a crow with this, 'HA HA?'"

Babs: "Glad you asked. Can you put it together? When do I do that annoying stuff?"

Sylvia: "Let see. I don't know. Oh yea, it's when I dump on myself."

Babs: "I wanted to pass something on to you but didn't want to sound preachy. I learned it the other day in my eating disorder group."

Sylvia: "Yeah, go on."

Babs: "When I said things like you said a moment ago, things that put myself down, like 'I can't do anything right,' my therapist said 'AH HA.' Of course, I got pissed and annoyed and said, 'Why don't you speak English? Stop this BS.' He explained that when I felt really bad, the next step was to figure out the automatic thought that led to the bad feeling. The point is not to criticize the thought, but to put it through the AH HA evidence test. Is the thought **Accurate**? Is the thought **Helpful**? See, AH HA. I thought that if I got you interested, even a little annoyed, you might ask what was going on, and I could share this with you. It really works for me."

Sylvia: "OK, let's try it out with the thought that I can't do anything right. Well, now that I think of it, I can do lots of things right. I take care of my cat. I'm patient with my little brat brother. I'm kind to grandma. So that thought is not *accurate*. And it sure is not *helpful*. It only makes me feel more down on myself. I like the idea of not stuffing my feelings or criticizing my thoughts. The idea of testing my thoughts lets me decide in a more grown up way which thoughts I want to keep and which I want to junk."

Babs: "That is so great. I'll stop this AH HA stuff if you promise to give it a try for a week."

Sylvia: "AH HA, HA HA."

Comment

The core of CBT is interrupting the direction of dysphoric moods into eating disordered behaviors. Instead, use the emotion as a smoke detector to ask, "What is the thought generating that crummy feeling?" Once the thought is identified—which takes practice because it is often automatic—ask of the thought: Is it Accurate? Is it Helpful? It's amazing how useful this testing of thoughts by a simple (maybe annoying) AH HA grid. Time and time again, once a patient with lots of dysphoria gets good at capturing the automatic thought generating the dysphoria, then I see a smile on their face when they say, "Yeah, that is not accurate. I've checked out the evidence. And it sure isn't helpful." The AH HA test applies to overvaluation of the benefits of thinness, self-critical views, and a pervasive sense of inefficacy, the core of anxiety. Yes, there are many more subtleties to CBT, but a good start is getting patients to apply AH HA to the thoughts generating dysphoria that used to get stuffed with eating disordered behaviors.

Originally published in 2011.

97

It's Hard to Say Goodbye

all ED, recovery tool, quality of life

Kent and Barb were each staring gloomily into their Diet Cokes.

"I sure miss Ed," said Barb. "He was always there for us. When no one else understood, he did. When he was around I knew what to do with my stress."

"Yeah, it's a bummer," said Kent. "When I was a fat, pimply junior in high school, Ed came to my rescue, too."

After a few more minutes of reminiscing, Alissa and Twyla stopped by. "Hey, what are you guys so down about?"

Once they explained it to the two new arrivals, Alissa and Twyla nodded in agreement. "It's sure hard to find loyal friends these days. And then when you lose one, the world is a lot scarier. Like, I'm going to a college across country this fall, and I don't know how I'll handle it."

Twyla chimed in, "Totally agree with you. I'm returning to professional dance school for the summer program. My treatment is over, but what will I do with all those mirrors?"

Brent joined the group. "OK, don't tell me. I know what you are talking about. You have been reading my mind. It's Ed. He's gone, left town, scooted, vamoosed. I'm so tempted to run after him, search the

Internet. I know if I asked him to come back, he would. After all, he's not dead, just gone away. Every once in a while, I imagine him telling me to remember to follow his plan."

Laurissa had finished her group therapy notes and was walking past the group. "Today was a graduation, not a wake, and here you all are looking like your best friend has passed. I'd like you to get back on track and remember the real Ed. Sure, Ed was always there—always there in a bad way. Each of you was trapped by Ed's confident advice that if you lost enough weight, or bulked up enough muscle, everything in life would go your way. No, you are not losing a friend. You are losing a noose, a strangler vine that wouldn't let you keep growing emotionally.

"Remember, today's unhealthy solutions become tomorrow's problems, whether it's drugs, eating disorders, or self-cutting. Your emotions went into the deep freeze. Now, you must learn to deal with them—hooray for emotions! Remember the exercises we did to cultivate positive emotions. We meant not only to kick Ed in the butt, not only to pick weeds, but to grow roses.

"After a couple of weeks of vacation for me, we'll resume the group therapy for anyone who is in the area. Hey, gang, I'm not scolding you. It's totally natural to miss someone who gave the illusion of help—it was a form of help, but very temporary, and with an enormous price tag. How about holding a passing-away service for Ed. Then we'll have a celebration for your new life—led by yourself. It's normal to mourn for Ed, but only for a bit. It's normal to be scared without his control. But you have yourself back on a healthy pattern of dealing with life, you have each other, you have your new buddies. It's time to say goodbye to Ed. Love you guys."

Comment

Eating disorders (Ed) are problem solvers, but even bigger problem givers. You would have to be a little bit nuts to say, "No, don't straighten my broken leg or don't take out my inflamed appendix." But eating disorders are different, and that is one reason why people in general don't understand that they are not simply a voluntary habit. Once developed, eating disorders have a life of their own. They do actually make some feelings better for a while. They allow a person to avoid making difficult decisions, deflect hurt feelings from unkind comments, and give the illusion of control. But then the price tag comes: developmental arrest, medical complications, self-isolation, relentless exercise, guilt, and poor relationships.

Many, not all, of our patients go through a period of time when they are improved in their eating disordered behavior, and are recognizing the true need of dealing with life's issues in healthy ways, but are not yet solid. This is the time when it is so tempting to call Ed back into the picture.

I have promised many patients that if they will sincerely commit to practicing healthy eating, thinking, and behaviors about food, weight, and shape for a year, and then can say they were truly happier with their eating disorder running their life, I would send a thousand dollars to their favorite charity. Guess what, I haven't lost a dime!

So, validate the sense of mourning that some patients have during their not-quite-solid phase of wellness, but go on to encourage working through the mourning and moving on to a life free of Ed.

Originally published in 2011.

98

Thermometers and Thermostats

all ED, recovery tool, quality of life

"Oh, I am so sleek and thin. Sometimes, I have a silver center surrounded by glass, like a glamorous piece of jewelry. And you know what silver costs these days! Otherwise, my center is red and people can't stop looking at me. Red never goes out of style—like brightening up a boring, black cocktail dress with a red handbag and shoes, or Marilyn Monroe's lipstick. I am so fashionable, people check me out every day—a thermometer. They want me. They need me."

"I can't argue with you. You certainly are glamorous—long and thin. I'm pretty clunky myself, usually rectangular or square. Nothing fancy about being beige or dull gray. Lots of times, people try to hide me. I'm a wallflower compared to you. I may only get looked at a couple of times a year. Then, someone pushes a few buttons on me, goes away, and I continue to gather dust for another six months."

"I feel sorry for you, my clunky thermostat friend. Wish I could do something for you. Oops, hold on. My silver-colored center just shot up. The sun is shining brightly on the terrace, where fabulous people are having cocktails, and they all keep staring at me. Believe me, I get plenty of attention."

"For a thermostat, I'm feeling a little happier for a change. My owner, a bearded guy who eats lots of granola and rides his bike everywhere, came up to me the other day and changed a few of the dials. He said, 'You know, little thermostat, you saved me hundreds of bucks last winter.' I may not be glamorous, but I do important work."

"Well, you still hardly ever get noticed. You are not thin and sleek. You don't have a silver or red center that goes up and down. Oops, excuse me for a moment. I suddenly shrunk to this little itty bitty thing, and I'm feeling very cold. Ouch, I fell! My silver center is running out. I'm being swept up and put in the trash. Help me. Help me. Help...."

And then there was silence.

Meanwhile, the thermostat continued to do his job day after day, changing the temperature cycle, switching from air conditioning to heat, turning the furnace on and off. Not very glamorous, but much valued.

Comment

In an interview in the *New York Times Sunday Magazine,* Professor Cornel West is quoted as saying "You've got to be a thermostat rather than a thermometer. A thermostat shapes the climate of opinion; a thermometer just reflects it." What a wonderful summary of the difference between thermometers and thermostats!

I encourage patients to become thermostats. Most patients with anorexia nervosa act like thermometers—when the fashion climate, or their friends, or the media say thin is in, they work to get slimmer. Hemlines up, hemlines down. And it's sad. So many fashion models only look glamorous when dressed up, but medically are starved and boney. Of course, guys follow trends and can be thermometers too—be leaner and more muscular.

In contrast, a person who is a thermostat sets the climate, doesn't follow it, or more accurately, doesn't follow it when it is unhealthy. The thermostat controls the temperature, while the thermometer simply follows the temperature set by the thermostat.

When the daughter of a friend of mine was eating a second hot dog during lunch with her dance team comrades, one friend said, "Ellie, you're going to get fat. That's your second hot dog. I wouldn't eat even one hot dog." Ellie calmly went on eating her second hot dog, and gently said to her teammate, "You know Liz, these hot dogs are surprisingly good. We work out hard and need to eat enough calories to maintain our strength for the games. I wonder if you might have an eating disorder, or the beginning of one. There's a friend of my dad who coordinates an eating disorders clinic. I'd be glad to give you his name. And, oh, I think I'll get that chocolate ice cream for dessert." Ellie was setting the climate, not following it.

When a patient learns to be a thermostat, not a thermometer, she or he becomes empowered to examine cultural trends, and then decide whether to follow them or not. More importantly, they let other people know (in a non-judgmental way) what they think and why they do what they do.

Kudos to Professor Cornel West for his summary of the difference between thermometers and thermostats. Goofy story, maybe. Important concept, yes.

Originally published in 2012.

99

It's War Over There—and Here

trauma, all ED, sexual abuse

Carla was an experienced Marine Corps sergeant who had seen service in Iraq and Afghanistan on three tours of duty. She was invited to the eating disorders evening group at the local community center to tell her story, because the group had helped her in the past. What a commanding presence she was: outfitted in desert camouflage gear, shoulders broad but feminine in her physique, with a squared-away appearance that engendered instant respect. On planes, passengers wanted to shake her hand and thank her. This is what she said: "Guys, it's war out there, and war is hell, but someone has to protect our country, even if you don't agree with every policy. I want to tell you a story that keeps me up at night to this day, and when I do sleep, I have nightmares. The VA is doing their best to help, and it's coming along, but slowly." Then, she told more about her experience of war.

> One day, we were in a small town in Afghanistan, being friendly with the locals to show them that we were on the side of peace. As we drove slowly through town, making stops to hand out diapers and vitamins to groups of young mothers and their children, we were on the lookout for IEDs—that's

improvised explosive devices, bombs. Toward the end of the town, I saw one of those damn IEDs on the side of the road—disguised as a tin can behind a clump of weeds. I knew my duty. I stopped the jeep and started to walk cautiously toward the IED to inspect it and see if we could either disable or move it, so it wouldn't do any harm. Can't believe what happened. A young girl, about 8 or 9, had been following our slowly moving jeep. She darted out ahead of me and picked up the IED. You know what happened. The blast shredded her body and threw me back against the jeep, concussed one of my buddies, and tore a hole in the face of another. When I came to my senses, I half-crawled over to what remained of the girl—only a few pieces of her yellow dress and a couple of shredded flowers she was trying to give me remained.

That's only one of the traumatic events that happened in Afghanistan, but the worst. I can't get it out of my mind. If only I had been faster in getting to it. If only I had seen her and warned her away. If only. But "if onlys" don't count. This precious little girl was gone forever. I wake up at night in a sweat dreaming of the explosion and trying to warn the girl. Every time I hear a car backfire, I hit the concrete instinctively. I break down when I see little girls in yellow dresses. No, I'm not going back to my eating disorder and this PTSD will eventually get better. But that's what war does to you. I am accepting another tour of duty, partly because I believe that women belong in the armed forces, in every role. Any thoughts?

After a few moments of silence, Leslie stood up and spoke with tears in her eyes, "What a story. But you know, Carla, it's war over here, too. I was raped at a party by someone I thought was a friend. I can't get it out of my mind either. I get the sweats at night and go right down to the refrigerator for a binge to settle down. I know it's not healthy, but these nightmares terrorize me. Sometimes, I don't even remember that I had a binge, except for the bulge in my stomach in the morning. And all those reminders during a regular day that trigger my memories, and I want to binge.

"Yeah," said Kyle, "I was at school and saw some guy pull out a gun and shoot our teacher and some of my classmates. I can't go to any movies now that have guns. And those sweats you are talking about. That's me. When the flashback comes, my heart feels like it's coming out of chest, it's beating so strongly. I feel hot and cold at the same time. The only thing that settles me down is to deny myself food and run for hours."

And so it went. When she was younger, Marie had been sexually assaulted in her own bedroom by an older cousin. It happened whenever her uncle's family came over. She just couldn't tell her parents. They would never believe it. She decided if she became so thin and boney that no one would be attracted to her, she would be safe; but she never felt safe, except in this therapy group.

Everyone gave Carla a big hug at the end of the group. They all realized they were there for each other. Bad things, really bad things, happen in foreign wars, but also in our own homes. The group made a decision to be more open about what happened to each one of them in the past, and to text each other if they were having a flashback. War is hell, wherever it happens.

Comment

Carla's is a true story told to me by a patient. To this day, she can't forget the trauma and violence in her deployments, but especially the tragedy with the little girl in the yellow dress. Whether trauma, sexual or other, is related to an increased chance of developing eating disorders is somewhat controversial. Now, after far too long, the military is getting honest about the high prevalence of PTSD in service personnel. At least a third of the eating disorders patients I have treated have had traumatic experiences and then relive the experiences. They vary from bad memories to a daily reliving of trauma, often triggered by innocuous stimuli. Most have night terrors, as well. For some of these patients, binge eating, dieting, or extreme exercise has become their "solution."

The methods of treating PTSD are still evolving, and generally improving. But certainly no history and examination of an eating disorders patient is complete without a detailed, compassionate, gentle inquiry into a history of trauma—and no, it should not be done at the first meeting, but only when trust is gained. Whether or not the trauma is directly related to the onset and maintenance of the eating disorder is not the point—identification and treatment of PTSD is a package deal in treating patients with eating disorders. There are no "Lone Rangers" when it comes to eating disorders—virtually all eating disorders come as package deals, and these days, PTSD, whether overseas or stateside, is too often part of the picture.

Originally published in 2013.

100

Togglers and Dimmers

all eating disorders, recovery tool, therapy

Once upon a time, there was a contest between a Toggler and a Dimmer for who had the greatest influence on the world. Now the Toggler lived in a world where everything was on or off, black or white, light or dark. The Toggle switch was always either all off or all on. He was very proud of his role in the modern world. In fact, he had international recognition. His name in French was *Le Toggleur*, and the Eiffel Tower could be instantly lit up after dark with a simple flip of his switch. In German, it was *Das Togglemeister*. And in Spanish, *Toggle Hombre*. The United Nations even considered celebrating an "International Toggle Day" with a Guinness prize for the fastest Toggle switch in the world.

"Not so fast," said the advocates for recognizing the role of Dimmers in the world. The Dimmer goes from *off* to *gradually on,* like a slide. "Most of human life and nature in general works on a Dimmer model," one expert said. When you want to test a new electronic signal, you start at a low energy level, and gradually increase the intensity until the full effect is realized. It is only on Mercury and a few other distant planets that day suddenly becomes night. Here, day becomes twilight, then night, and then dawn gradually arrives. The French call Dimmers *les amants*, the lovers, because of their similarity to lovers who show gradual growing passion. The Germans call them *langsam schnell* or "slow fast," and every beer hall in Bavaria begins and ends the evening with songs to the Dimmers of the World, who bring forth the nuances of life with subtlety and flexibility.

And so the debate continued regarding which was more important, the Togglers or the Dimmers. Finally, a wise, older woman, a Doula in fact, who had helped deliver thousands of babies, finally spoke some wisdom to achieve reconciliation. "You know," she said, "some kids burst out into the world like a rocket from their mommy's tummies in minutes, others emerge slowly over hours; and, both grow up to contribute to the world."

She also had counseled hundreds of young people with eating disorders over the years, often young people she had delivered. She told everyone who would listen that some patients with anorexia nervosa "get it" after just a few days of treatment, catching on quickly to cognitive behavioral therapy. They come to understand that their drive for thinness and overvaluation of body size and shape is a way to deal with emotions, development, and relationships. These are the Togglers.

Other anorexic patients need to have their weight restored to an almost fully-healthy weight, sometimes months after they enter treatment, before therapy makes much sense. These are the Dimmers, whose brains only gradually light up, who start practicing normal patterns of thinking and acting in a healthy manner only slowly, but then they truly "get it" as they continue their progress after more time in treatment, and thereafter.

The Togglers react quickly and strongly with their emotions, while the Dimmers gradually become aware of their feelings. "Therefore," the wise woman said, "let the Togglers and the Dimmers be at peace with each other. Let the treatment teams respect and work equally intensively and empathetically with both kinds of people. Love them both and treat them all according to their needs."

Comment:

At times, treatment teams become frustrated with Dimmer patients who seem slow to "get it" and ask the same questions over and over: "How much weight do I need to gain?" "Aren't I fat enough already?" "My stomach is already so big." Then, there are Togglers, who we need to avoid idealizing and seeing as "darlings" of treatment. They seem to get everything right away, are compliant, and appear to be "insightful." Only time will tell whether these Togglers will become and stay healthier than the Dimmers, who catch on slowly.

Treatment teams should consider that it is important not to favor in subtle ways those patients who seem to "get it" quickly. Some may truly be Togglers, who come along quickly, while others may simply be good at giving answers they know will please the staff (pseudo-Togglers), but have only intellectual insight. If a particular subject has difficulty learning in the beginning and catches on slowly, there is no indication that less mastery will result.

Brain studies show a frustrating variability in the degree of ventricular enlargement and the amount of decreased cortical gray matter in anorexic patients of similar severe weight loss. How much the starved brain will recover remains to be seen as long-term outcome studies are carried out; but in general, the ventricular dilatation decreases, and the gray matter increases in mass as patients restore weight. But whether there is any correlation between those who get it quickly (the Togglers) and those who come along slowly (the Dimmers) remains unknown. There are no outcome studies regarding whether Togglers or Dimmers do better in the long run.

Originally published in 2013.

101

Jeanette's Feast

all eating disorders, recovery tool, family dynamics, quality of life

Jeanette thought her anorexia was the secret to a happy life. It gave her a sense of security, identity, and control. Having moved to the Midwest from France as a small child, she dreaded the major holidays, when her family celebrated with an abundance of the kinds of tasty foods she resisted. For July 4th, there'd be no hot dogs, hamburgers, or German potato salad for her; no chocolate cake with an American flag on top, no matter how yummy it looked. Her no-fat cottage cheese was more than plenty. Thank you very much. Thanksgiving was the worst, what an indulgence—for her to avoid.

Jeanette had grown taller, but by age 15 she still had not developed regular monthly cycles. Her mother took her to the pediatrician to find out what was going on, and after an assessment, the doctor explained, "Well, Jeanette, you have anorexia nervosa. It comes from an overvaluation of thinness. I wouldn't be surprised if you think you are a little overweight and want to take off some pounds."

"You must be reading my mind," she replied, "but I like being thinner."

"Jeanette, I'd like you to see one of my colleagues, Dr. Hasan, who is a very good psychologist. She's warm and likes teens."

So, grudgingly at first, but eventually with more insight and enthusiasm, Jeanette bonded with Dr. Hasan and came to see how dreadfully thin she was. After about six months, her recovery had progressed brilliantly. She had just about reached a healthy weight, and began to see Dr. Hasan every other week, and a year later, once a month. "I can't believe I didn't see what this self-starvation was all about," she admitted. "Now, I like myself; and, there's something important I want to do for my family."

For the French Feast of the 3 Kings, also called Twelfth Night, she planned a very special desert: a *galette des Rois*, a rich cake traditionally served only on that holiday. It contained lots of almond paste, chocolate, and fruits; and, hidden inside was a small crown that would be prized by the lucky person who found it in their slice. Her family rarely celebrated this day in the U.S., so they didn't suspect a thing. Jeanette secretly assembled the ingredients at a friend's house, even the little symbols that go on top of the cake, as well as the crown for inside.

She also prepared a whole feast meal to serve them: scallops in cream for the first course, followed by a lean filet mignon with a mushroom and butter sauce, tiny French green beans, and escalloped potatoes with cheese on top. A meal that would have terrified her to eat in the past, she was delighted to serve and enjoy. Her surprised family was blown away, but more was to come. After the salad course (always served after the entrée), she turned the lights down. Then, while humming a French tune, she carried in the *galette des Rois,* with candles on top—the kind you can't blow out (the French might not approve but who cares)—and placed it in the center of the table. She didn't notice the tears of joy in her mother's eyes.

"My loving family," she began, "you have been so supportive through my ordeal with anorexia. Thank you *mille fois* (a thousand times). I'm over it for good! I wanted to mark my recovery with you on this special feast day, in our French tradition. From now on, the Feast of the 3 Kings will also be 'Jeanette's Feast Day,' and count on me to make the cake. I love you all." As they delighted in the delicious *galette*, no one was surprised when Jeanette bit into the tiny crown.

Comment:

What a misery it is for patients with anorexia nervosa to attend festive meals—not binges, but good, old-fashioned feasts—whether American, French, or from any tradition. Usually a person with anorexia nervosa avoids the event entirely, or cooks up a storm and then doesn't eat. What a triumph of the recovery process to be able to partake with glee. You might want to see the classic film, *Babette's Feast*, about a poor French woman who emigrates to Denmark (subtitles) and finally finds the money to throw a feast for the family that has sheltered her. No one is shot, no galactic invaders. But once you get used to the measured pace, and the great feast is finally served, the viewer practically becomes a participant with the reserved community who discover what a feast is truly about—a celebration of love and sharing.

Originally published in 2015.

Index of Keywords

(Numbers correspond to stories, not pages)

About the Authors

Arnold Andersen, MD

Professor Emeritus, University of Iowa Carver College of Medicine and adjunct lecturer at Johns Hopkins Medical School, Andersen is the world's leading authority on eating disorders in men. For over 15 years, he was the director of the eating disorders program at the University of Iowa College of Medicine and a professor of Psychiatry. He founded the first inpatient eating disorders program at the Johns Hopkins Department of Psychiatry under the direction of Paul McHugh. In addition to treating patients and teaching, he has written several texts and has contributed more than 200 articles in scientific publications. He has also lectured widely to medical and psychological groups worldwide. Dr. Andersen has appeared on a number of national television programs in which he has discussed eating disorders and he has been quoted in numerous publications, including the *Wall Street Journal, Newsweek*, and the *New York Times.*

Leigh Cohn, MAT, CEDS

Leigh Cohn, MAT, CEDS is the Publisher of Gürze Books, Editor-in-Chief of *Eating Disorders: The Journal of Treatment and Prevention*, and coauthor of more than a dozen books, including two on eating disorders and males, *Making Weight* (2000) and *Current Findings on Males and Eating Disorders* (2014), and the first book ever published on bulimia (1980). He has spoken at professional conferences and universities throughout North America, and has received awards from the International Association of Eating Disorders Professionals, the Eating Disorders Coalition, and the National Eating Disorders Association, of which he is a member of the Founders Council.